Published in 2016 by:
Helion & Company Limited
26 Willow Road
Solihull
West Midlands
B91 1UE
England
Tel. 0121 705 3393
Fax 0121 711 4075
email: info@helion.co.uk
website: www.helion.co.uk
Twitter: @helionbooks
Visit our blog http://blog.helion.co.uk/

Text © Leopold Scholtz 2016
Maps drawn by and © Camille Burger
Photographs © SANDF Archives

Designed & typeset by Farr out Publications,
    Wokingham, Berkshire
Cover design by Paul Hewitt, Battlefield
    Design (www.battlefield-design.co.uk)
Printed by Henry Ling Ltd, Dorchester,
    Dorset

ISBN 978-1-909384-62-0

British Library Cataloguing-in-Publication
    Data
A catalogue record for this book is available
    from the British Library

Cover: Tanks advancing at full speed during
an exercise in the Free State in 1988.

CONTENTS

PREFACE

During most of the years of the Border War, I was a journalist at *Die Burger*, an Afrikaans-language Cape Town newspaper. We journalists knew more about what went on in the war in South West Africa (now Namibia) and the South African military involvement in Angola than the average person in the street. But we did not know all that much more, and what we knew, we could not publish without the permission of the South African Defence Force (SADF) – which was not forthcoming with information at all.

What we heard from the other side, SWAPO, the Angolan MPLA government and Fidel Castro's Cuba, was unadulterated propaganda. I remember well a press conference in the Netherlands in the late seventies when Sam Nujoma, leader of SWAPO, claimed that his forces had attacked and wiped out an entire South African infantry battalion in the north of SWA. One should only read his memoirs[1] to see the pure drivel emanating from that side.

Having qualified myself as a military historian with a PhD, this frustrated me no end. Even then, I longed for a businesslike analysis in which propaganda and political partisanship would play no role. Alas, after war's end, the political posturing – with notable exceptions – continued. Politicians, ex-soldiers and even academics from whom one would expect better, continued the war, taking sides and fighting about who won the war.[2]

1 Sam Nujoma: *Where Others Wavered. The Autobiography of Sam Nujoma* (London, Panaf, 2001).
2 See Leopold Scholtz: "The standard of research on the Battle of Cuito Cuanavale, 1987-1988" (*Scientia Militaria*, 39/1, 2011, pp. 115-137).

In the end, I wrote my own history of the war, *The SADF in the Border War 1966-1989* (published by Tafelberg in 2013 and Helion in 2015). In that book, I believe I called it as the sources dictated, without fear of favour.

But that book is over 500 pages long. It goes into considerable detail, perhaps too much for the average person whose interest in a far-off conflict is not that intense. So, when I was asked to do a much shorter book about the so-called Battle of Cuito Cuanavale, the climax right at the end of the war, I jumped at the chance. In this little book, readers will find a much shorter analysis of the war, especially of the final nine months. I also try to answer the question who won the battle, without descending into propaganda myself.

I should perhaps declare my personal interest. I am an ex-reservist soldier who received my military training in 1966 at the Army Gymnasium, a unit which was then regarded as an elite infantry battalion, taking in only volunteers. I then served with the Citizen Force Regiment University of Stellenbosch until the end of 1975, when my service was up. This was exactly when the war started hotting up. I was again recruited for the post-apartheid South African National Defence Force, with whom I served as a reservist staff officer (Captain) in various positions until my retirement.

Above all, however, I am a professional military historian who take my craft very seriously. Truth is what I try to serve, not politics. Whether I have succeeded, is, of course, for others to decide.

INTRODUCTION

Seldom in modern history has there been a military campaign so hotly contested in public memory as the one known as the Battle of Cuito Cuanavale. In this campaign elements of the South African Defence Force (SADF), allied with the Angolan rebel movement UNITA, fought against FAPLA, the Marxist Angolan MPLA government's defence force, as well as the Cuban military. Under Soviet guidance, FAPLA launched a huge offensive in August-September 1987 from the village of Cuito Cuanavale southwards to eliminate UNITA, but was stopped on the banks of the Lomba River by SADF units. Together with reinforcements, these then embarked on a counteroffensive in which FAPLA was driven back far northwards, until the Angolans retained only a smallish bridge-head at Tumpo, on the eastern bank of the Cuito River and opposite Cuito Cuanavale itself. There, the final SADF attempts to dislodge the Angolans were rebuffed. And then, far to the west, the Cubans started advancing menacingly southwards toward the South West African (SWA) border, creating uncertainty in the SADF high command that SWA might be invaded.

At the same time, peace talks were started and, with American mediation, these led to the peace accord signed in New York in December 1988.

These are the bare, uncontested facts of Operations Moduler, Hooper and Packer, as they were known in the SADF, Saludando Octubre (the FAPLA name, referring to the October 1917 Revolution in Russia) or Maniobra XXXI Aniversario del Decembarco del Granma (as the Cubans called their contribution, referring to the

first landing of Fidel Castro and his guerrilla band in 1956 on the shores of Cuba). But there the consensus ends. Ever since 1988 a furious battle of words has been fought between those who maintain that the SADF achieved a glorious victory, and those who say that the SADF met its nemesis and that this heralded the final downfall of the hated apartheid regime. Among those sympathetic to FAPLA and the Cubans, there has even been talk of South Africa's "Stalingrad",[3] evoking memories of an enormous blood-bath among the South Africans and a humiliating surrender.

These claims have been hugely exaggerated on both sides. Nevertheless, there is a common thread in these opposing interpretations. The "anti-South Africans", if one may use that term, emphasise the fact that the SADF in the end was repulsed at the Tumpo bridgehead during the final weeks of the campaign and that they could not take Cuito Cuanavale. They largely ignore the significance of the rest of the campaign. The South Africans themselves emphasise the victories at the Lomba River and downplay the Tumpo reverses. In fact, one SADF officer, the late Brigadier-General J.N.R. ("Junior") Botha – during the campaign he was a Colonel and Senior Staff Officer: Operations at Army HQ – even maintained that there never was a "Battle of Cuito Cuanavale".[4]

3 *See* Isaac Saney: "African Stalingrad: The Cuban revolution, internationalism and the end of apartheid" (*Latin American Perspectives*, 33/81, 2006).
4 Junior Botha: "Samevatting van Operasies Moduler, Hooper en Packer", in Jannie Geldenuys (ed.): *Ons was Daar. Wenners van die Oorlog om Suider-Afrika* (Pretoria, Kraal, 2013), p. 413.

Of course, a lot depends on the question whether the SADF indeed wanted to take Cuito Cuanavale. If they did, and failed, one may reason that they were defeated. If they didn't, this assertion becomes much more difficult.

It is clear that they cannot all be correct. In fact, this debate, which may even be called a "Second Battle of Cuito Cuanavale", makes the impression that many participants are less concerned with the historical facts than with scoring ideological points or with defending reputations. However, a serious historian cannot be overly concerned with either politics or reputations. He must try

and uncover the unvarnished truth. This is the purpose of this little book. Whether I have succeeded, is, of course, not for me to say.

Two final points: This analysis is largely based on a book I published recently, *The SADF in the Border War 1966-1989*. It is, however, not a simple summary. I have tried to rethink the whole history afresh. Secondly, in the course of this work, I refer to the territory today known as Namibia with the old name, South West Africa or SWA. This has nothing to do with any political persuasion on my part; it is merely because that was the official name of the territory before it became independent in 1990.

CHAPTER 1
BACKGROUND

The campaign which culminated in the conventional clashes between the Lomba River and the Tumpo bridgehead in 1987-1988 did not fall out of the sky. In order to properly understand what went on there, we will have to identify several strands of the background and then weave them together.

Firstly, the Border War – the South African umbrella name for the conflict of which the Battle of Cuito Cuanavale formed the final act – in fact consisted of several wars, all rolled into one. First of all, it was an anti-colonial liberation war, fought by the South West African People's Organisation (SWAPO) against South African domination. Secondly, it was also a war against the South African policy of *apartheid* – enforced racial separation – which was experienced by blacks as being racist. This part of the war manifested itself in a classic counterinsurgency war, fought by SWAPO guerrillas and the SADF, south of the Angolan border. Finally, it was part of the Cold War, especially when the Cubans were drawn in as well. This last element of the conflict was fought out in southern Angola, in the form of several SADF operations against SWAPO's back areas, as well as against the Angolan and Cuban armies. It took the form of highly mobile, mechanised operations.

The early war
The war started in August 1966, when a force of South African paratroopers and policemen swooped on a SWAPO base at Ongulumbashe in Ovamboland. (Notwithstanding propaganda, this was the only military base the movement ever had in SWA.) In the early years, SWAPO was politically and militarily based in Zambia. To reach SWA, insurgents had to move through Angola, still a Portuguese colony, which proved a considerable impediment. However, in April 1974, a military coup d'etat in Lisbon removed the fascist dictatorship and paved the way for Angola and other Portuguese colonies in Africa to become independent.

This meant a drastic improvement in SWAPO's strategic position. Now the insurgents could set up safe bases just across the border in neighbouring Angola, a factor which is often a prerequisite for a successful guerrilla war. And indeed, within a short time SWAPO bands swarmed all over the north of SWA, and the SADF found itself in trouble.

An unwilling South African Government was persuaded by several African states (as well as nods and winks from Washington, paralysed by the final American humiliation in Vietnam just months before) to intervene in Angola to prevent the Marxist MPLA liberation movement from taking over the territory in the ensuing

civil war. Several SADF motorised columns, supported by armoured cars and artillery, raced northward from October 1975 to enable the other two liberation movements, FNLA and UNITA, to occupy as much territory as possible. The idea was to put them in a strong negotiation position vis-a-vis the MPLA. But it became a political and strategic debacle. The Soviet Union, as well as Cuba's dictator, Fidel Castro, started sending military aid to the MPLA towards the end of 1974, long before South Africa's intervention. But when the SADF columns started racing northwards, the Communists – wrongly, as it turned out – feared that the purpose was to chase out the MPLA from Luanda. This was indeed debated behind the scenes in South Africa, but the powers that be decided against it because of the expected high casualties. (This was the first of several mutual misunderstandings, lasting throughout the conflict. We shall see them returning during the Battle of Cuito Cuanavale as well.) Fidel Castro then intervened on a grand scale, moving thousands of troops to Angola, where they soon tangled with the SADF in several bloody clashes. South Africa's international support evaporated, and the Government decided to cut its losses and pull out, in spite of the impressive tactical and operational success of the fighting troops at the front.

This not only resulted in a massive loss of political face for South Africa, but SWAPO immediately exploited the new situation. The SWAPO fighters surged in great numbers over the border. Reading SADF documents and eyewitness accounts of the time, one is struck by the helplessness the South African military felt in the face of insurgents being indistinguishable from the local population, attacking isolated patrols and bases where and when they wanted. The SADF's large-scale sweeps were clumsy and achieved practically nothing. At this stage, SWAPO ran rings around the SADF.

Turn-around
However, things were about to change. In 1977, a new Commanding General was appointed in Windhoek, SWA's capital. He was Major-General Jannie Geldenhuys, who later became Chief of the Army and Chief of the Defence Force. Although he – like other senior South African officers – had no operational experience, Geldenhuys had an excellent understanding of higher strategy and counterinsurgency warfare. He reorganised the SADF's war effort accordingly in several ways.

South of the border, the emphasis was moved away from South African white conscripts – often city boys who didn't understand the physical and cultural environment – to native troops, mostly

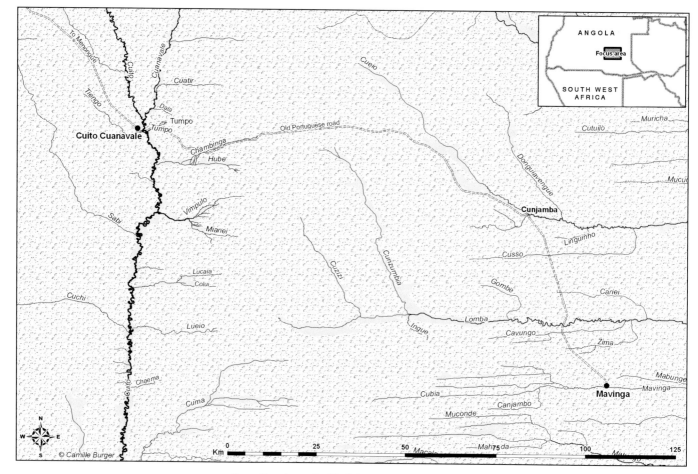

Operational area for Moduler, Hooper and Packer.

Ovambos and Bushmen who knew the vicinity and the people intimately. The operational area was deluged by infantry patrols to show the flag, as it were. When these chanced upon insurgents, they would radio for reinforcements from nearby bases. There, so-called Romeo Mike units (*reaksiemag* in Afrikaans, or "reaction force") would be flown in by Puma helicopter, sometimes dropped with parachutes, or else charged to the scene in Casspir armoured personnel carriers. Together with air support from converted Alouette III helicopter gunships, equipped with 20 mm side-firing cannon, this was more often than not sufficient to win virtually every single clash, killing or wounding many insurgents and forcing the others to flee back to Angola.

This was coupled with a massive civil action campaign to build roads, schools and clinics in order to win the hearts and minds of the local population. Winning the locals' hearts and minds became a central element of the South African counterinsurgency doctrine. In Ovamboland, SWAPO's main support base, this had only limited success, as the Ovambos continued to see SWAPO as "our" boys and the SADF as the occupiers. In the ethnically unrelated Okavangoland, Caprivi and Kaokoland more success was booked.

At the same time, *apartheid* was progressively dismantled in SWA, removing it as a *casus belli*.

Indeed, SADF statistics show how the South Africans (militarily, that is) handsomely won the counterinsurgency war. The number of SWAPO guerrillas in northern SWA dwindled. Firefights were overwhelmingly initiated by the SADF, indicating that the South Africans were dominating the battlefield. The number of mines detected went up dramatically, and those exploding went down.

But there was also another – crucial – element in the South African strategy. Geldenhuys realised that it made no sense to wait passively

south of the border until the insurgents crossed it and started creating mayhem. This meant that the enemy held the initiative, and that was no way for South Africa to win the war. Therefore, he recommended to the SADF high command to start huge cross-border operations in Angola to disrupt SWAPO's infiltrations before they could take place and to attack the movement's bases in its rear areas.

The first such operation was the controversial parachute attack on Cassinga deep in Angola (which, by the way, was demonstrably not the innocent refugee centre alleged by SWAPO propaganda) and a mechanised attack on the SWAPO base of Chetequera just across the border in May 1978. The Cassinga attack turned on a knife-edge and was never repeated, but the Chetequera operation became the template for all subsequent operations into Angola. The biggest ones were Rekstok and Saffraan (1979), Sceptic (1980), Protea and Daisy (1981), Super, Makro and Meebos I and II (1982), and Askari (1983-1984).

In this way, slowly but surely, the SADF started getting the upper hand from 1980 onwards. SWAPO was forced back about 250 km into Angola, and the insurgents had to walk, heavily loaded with weapons, ammunition, mines and food, through an area dominated (though not always occupied) by the SADF. If they survived this harrowing experience, more SADF patrols were awaiting them in SWA. By 1988, their presence would become known within a few days, and they mostly did not last long before being either neutralised or forced to flee back across the border.

South Africa is sucked in

As time marched on, however, there were two closely interrelated developments which led to the climactic events of 1987-1988. First, as the SADF mechanised forces swarmed over southern Angola and disrupted SWAPO's plans, the insurgents turned to FAPLA, the MPLA's army, for protection, and got it. From 1981 onwards, therefore, in order to get at SWAPO, the SADF often had to forcefully push FAPLA out of the way first. The South Africans did not have any interest in fighting the MPLA government in Luanda as such. Their primary concern and objective was SWAPO, and FAPLA was only assaulted when it barred the way. But, by the early eighties, it seemed at times as if South Africa and Angola were at war.

Secondly, after the FNLA was practically eliminated in 1976, there was a civil war in Angola between the MPLA (supported by the Soviet Union and Cuba) and UNITA, supported by South Africa.

It is perhaps necessary to briefly outline the South African security strategy at this stage in order to understand its involvement in Angola. The South African government had already accepted independence as such for SWA in the second half of the seventies. But it was not willing to hand over power to SWAPO, which it viewed as a Communist proxy of the Soviet Union and Cuba. Therefore, the purpose was to create a situation in which that movement would lose an election, even if that took place under auspices of the United Nations. Acquiring political power through the barrel of a gun would also have been a major boost for the African National Congress (ANC) in its struggle in South Africa.

In April 1981, speaking to Reagan Administration officials, Defence Minister Magnus Malan (according to the officials' notes which were leaked to the press)

flatly declared that the [South African Government] can't accept prospects of a SWAPO victory which brings Soviet/Cuban forces to Walvis Bay. This would result from any election which left SWAPO in a dominant position. Therefore a SWAPO victory would be unacceptable in the context of a Westminster-type political system. [South Africa] does not rule out an internationally acceptable settlement, but could not live with a SWAPO victory that left SWAPO unchecked power.[5]

In similar vein, Pik Botha explained to the Americans during a visit by Haig's Deputy Secretary of State, Dick Clark, to South Africa in 1981, that his government was not against independence for Namibia as such. But

SWAPO must not be allowed to win an election in South West Africa. We were not prepared to exchange a war on the Kunene for a war on the Orange … If South West Africa would be governed by SWAPO, then a serious risk would rise that the Russians could threaten South Africa from the Territory. South Africa would then have to decide to invade the Territory in order to protect its interests. Such a situation would probably be less acceptable to the USA than the status quo. If SWAPO would govern South West Africa, Botswana would directly feel threatened, dr. Savimbi would be eliminated and South Africa would be totally encircled with Russian-inspired powers. If the entire Southern Africa then came under Russian tyranny, the strategic sea route around the Cape and its critical minerals would be lost to the West.[6]

Against this background, the SADF military strategy was to limit the insurgency as far as possible to the relatively small area of Ovamboland, SWAPO's main support base which housed almost half of the SWA population. The SADF's civic action programme helped to eliminate the insurgency to a great extent from Kavangoland, Caprivi and Kaokoland. This facilitated the counterinsurgency campaign. But the fact that UNITA occupied the entire southeastern corner of Angola also helped, as this made SWAPO's infiltration into Kavangoland and Caprivi in the northeastern regions of SWA very difficult, if not impossible. It was, therefore, in South Africa's strategic interest to keep UNITA alive and kicking. UNITA's downfall would have dealt a devastating blow to South Africa's war effort against SWAPO.

Nevertheless, South Africa did not want to get sucked into the Angolan civil war beyond aiding UNITA with weapons, logistical help and training. But, as wars are apt to do, the conflict escalated. A pattern developed which was important if one wants to understand the opening shots of the big campaign of 1987.

In 1983, the Government grudgingly gave permission to the SADF to use Buccaneer bombers and a 120 mm mortar battery to aid UNITA in capturing Cangamba, a central Angolan garrison town. In 1985 and 1986, they unleashed the new G-5 155 mm guns and Valkiri 127 mm rocket systems to help UNITA defend Mavinga against two somewhat chaotic FAPLA offensives. The South African Air Force (SAAF) also weighed in, while the Navy and Special Force operatives cooperated to sink several Soviet and Cuban freighters unloading supplies for the 1986 offensive in the harbour town of Namibe in a daring operation.

Thus a pattern evolved: All these operations were limited, short in duration, clandestine and plausibly deniable. The SADF seemed to get away with it each time. This was, therefore, the mind-set of the generals in Pretoria when the first reports of another looming FAPLA offensive started filtering in during the first months of 1987. If we are to understand the fateful decisions made before the fighting started, we need to keep this in the front of our minds.

The main adversaries

We may conclude this chapter with a few words about the main adversaries appearing in our story.

While the SADF was mostly unprepared for war when the conflict broke out in 1966, during the seventies and eighties it grew into a ferocious tactical force, greatly feared and respected by its opponents. New weapons systems were developed or existing ones upgraded. These included the highly mobile Ratel Infantry Fighting Vehicle (carrying a section of infantry and armed with a rapid-firing 20 mm gun), the one system without which the South Africans would never have been able to capture the initiative in the war.

Major-General Roland de Vries, who played a prominent role in developing the Ratel and the tactical and operational doctrine according to which the system was used, described it thus:

The Ratel's primary role in fighting of this kind was to carry troops swiftly in and out of battle, and it was admirably suited for this purpose because it provided all the required mobility, fire-power and armoured protection required for such combat conditions. High mobility combined with flexibility was the essence of this mobile war-fighting game.[7]

He goes on, saying "that the Ratel could close with enemy formations under own heavy indirect fire support, whilst being

5 Jaster: *The Defence of White Power. South African Policy under Pressure* (New York, St. Martin, 1988), p. 104.

6 Quoted in Leopold Scholtz: *The SADF in the Border War 1966-1989* (Solihull, Helion, 2015).

7 Roland de Vries: "Mobile warfare the African way – more in the mind and spirit than on paper" (unpublished article, 2015).

protected against own and enemy shrapnel, due to adequate armour protection."[8]

There also was a very successful armoured car version with a 90 mm gun, as well as a mobile 81 mm mortar version, enabling a balanced mechanised force to move rapidly across difficult terrain. In addition, two of the world's best artillery pieces, the 155 mm G-5 gun and the 127 mm Valkiri rocket system, were introduced during the eighties, enabling the South Africans to kill the enemy from up to 39 and 27 km, compared to the 23 km of the Soviet D-30 gun. The Centurion tank was upgraded with extra armour, a 105 mm gun, a new suspension and a diesel engine. This Olifant tank, as it was called, was more than a match for the T-54/55 encountered on the other side and was in fact developed to counter even the more advanced T-62.

Most importantly, since the middle sixties, the SADF developed a new conventional operational and tactical doctrine, honed for the African battleground. It rested on a mix of extreme mobility, surprise, aggressiveness, doing the unexpected and being unorthodox. Posession of ground as such was seen as irrelevant, unless it provided a tactical advantage. Typically, the enemy would be lured into a killing ground and destroyed there. Young officers such as Roland de Vries, Deon Ferreira, Tony Savides, Paul Fouché, Jan Malan, Koos Liebenberg and others developed and practiced the doctrine to perfection.

Roland de Vries became the foremost proponent of this doctrine, and practised it as OC 61 Mechanised Battalion Group (61 Mech) during Operations Protea and Daisy (1981). He wrote a book in Afrikaans, *Mobiele Oorlogvoering* ("Mobile Warfare", 1987) in which he expounded it at length.

Unfortunately, as we shall see, his book was apparently not read or sufficiently understood by his superiors. General Jannie Geldenhuys, Chief of the SADF, had an excellent understanding of war on the security and military strategic level, but his decisions during the Battle of Cuito Cuanavale suggest that this was not so much the case on the conventional operational level. The Chief of the Army, Lieutenant-General "Kat" Liebenberg, had a Special Forces background, and his utterances during the battle leads one to believe that his understanding of conventional operations was rather limited. The GOC SWA in Windhoek, Major-General Willie Meyer, functioned largely as a post office box between the front on the one hand and the Army and SADF headquarters in Pretoria on the other. He was not seen as a competent strategist or tactician by those serving under him.

The SADF also had a well-functioning command-and-control doctrine. Reading SADF documents, one is struck how battle plans contain only the bare outlines. Subordinate commanders were carefully informed about the objective and how they fitted into the broader plan. But beyond that, they were expected to think on their feet and take initiative when (not if!) confronted with unexpected obstacles. As long as they stayed within the parameters laid down by their superiors, they normally got all the scope to act independently.

While UNITA's guerrilla capabilities were uncontested, the South Africans never had a very high regard for their conventional ability. SADF members learned to distrust every piece of intelligence UNITA passed on, as this was often wrong or misleading. UNITA's charismatic but egocentric leader, Jonas Savimbi, tried hard to garner all credit for the SADF's battlefield successes, but did not succeed well.

On the other side of the hill, FAPLA was well equipped with T-54/55 tanks, D-30 guns, BM-21 (the famous "Stalin organ") rocket systems, etc. But it was a rather clumsy and chaotic force, more at ease in static defence than with mobile, offensive warfare. During the greater part of the Battle of Cuito Cuanavale it was led by a Soviet officer, Lieutenant-General Pyotr Gusev, with Soviet advisors down to battalion level. The ordinary soldiers were often pressed into service and did not understand – or care about – the MPLA's cause. Although individual units sometimes fought with surprising tenacity, in general FAPLA folded every time the South Africans made contact with them.

Finally the Cubans, who figured only in the latter stages of the battle, were much better organised and led, and much more aggressive than their Angolan counterparts. They also were somewhat inexperienced and rash, and this showed in their clashes with the South Africans. Nevertheless, one daresay that the SADF was rather shaken when discovering that the Cubans were much more efficient than FAPLA, although the South Africans gave as good as they got.

In contrast with the SADF, FAPLA and the Cubans' command-and-control doctrine was very rigid. Following their Soviet ideological mentors, battle plans were meant to be carried out to the smallest detail. Subordinate commanders got very little scope for independent initiative.

However, the war ended before the SADF and the Cubans could really get to grips with each other.

---

8 Ibid.

CHAPTER 2
INTO THE FRAY

From January 1987 onwards, South African intelligence became aware of a FAPLA build-up in the vicinity of Menongue and Cuito Cuanavale in the southeastern Angolan province of Cuando Cubango. It was confirmed early in March by Special Force operatives reporting from deep inside Angola. This build-up was the outcome of a clash of opinions between the Soviet and Cuban headquarters in Luanda. The Cubans had advised the Angolans to wage a patient, classic counterinsurgency war against UNITA, while the aggressive Russians wanted to knock out the rebel movement through a big conventional offensive with overwhelming force. It resulted in the two offensives of 1985 and 1986, starting in Cuito Cuanavale and moving southwards with the purpose of capturing the airstrip at Mavinga. This would then act as a springboard for capturing UNITA's headquarters at Jamba, after which, it was thought, the rebels would be finished.

Both offensives failed, South Africa having given clandestine military aid to UNITA. Now history seemed to be repeating itself. Carried out without any imagination, the 1987 offensive – Operation Saludando Octubre ("Salute to October", a reference to the October revolution of 1917 in tsarist Russia) – would follow the

The hulk of a destroyed Angolan T-54 or T-55 tank. The difference between the two models was marginal.

The same tank photographed from the front. The open hatches indicate that at least some of the crew got out alive.

A map of the operational area. Maps like these were used to plan tactics and operations, and also to explain battle plans to the officers and men.

An SADF officer explains a coming battle plan to his officers inside a camouflaged conference space. Because of the Angolan/Cuban mastery of the air, the South Africans had to rely heavily on camouflage nets like these. They worked extremely well.

same route.

On the South African side, the same predicament as in 1983, 1985 and 1986 existed, as explained in the previous chapter. The Government did not want to become embroiled in the Angolan civil war as such. But they felt they had to, in order to keep UNITA alive so that the movement could continue acting as a shield against SWAPO incursions into Kavangoland and Caprivi. Once again, the decision was to intervene in a short, limited and plausibly deniable fashion.

It is necessary to digress here for a moment. By 1987 South Africa's position was very difficult. At home, there was a full-scale insurrection in the townships, led by the ANC. A lot of the SADF's manpower had to be diverted there to keep the lid on. Internationally, the country was more isolated than ever before, and sanctions and boycotts on almost every terrain were sapping the white population's self-confidence.

Objectively speaking, South Africa could at this stage not afford a large-scale, open-ended conventional operation of any considerable length. In accordance with the lessons learnt from the politically

catastrophical invasion of Angola in 1975, all subsequent cross-border operations were short, sharp and with clearly defined political and military objectives. However, things would be very different this time.

The SADF reaction

The Angolan offensive started on 14 August, advancing ponderously southwards from Tumpo, just east of the Cuito River from Cuito Cuanavale. Once again, the idea was a grand conventional offensive to knock UNITA out of the war. As a leading member of the MPLA government afterwards explained, "If we went to the heart of the enemy, if we destroyed its headquarters at Jamba, then we would have practically won the war. This was a very seductive idea."[9] Of course, in order to get to Jamba, the airstrip at Mavinga had to be occupied first.

The FAPLA force consisted of eight brigades, of which four

9   Piero Gleijeses: *Visions of Freedom. Havana, Washington, Pretoria and the Struggle for Southern Africa* (Chapel Hill, University of Northern Carolina University Press, 2013), p. 394.

A Ratel-90 on the move in the Angolan bush. During the first weeks of Operation Moduler, these vehicles were utilised as *ersatz* tanks, taking on FAPLA tanks in spite of SADF doctrine specifying that tanks had to be used against tanks. South Africa only brought in tanks in the latter half of October 1987.

Assorted FAPLA vehicles stand around chaotically on the battlefield after the pitched battle of 3 October 1987, when 61 Mechanised Battalion Group obliterated the Angolan 47 Brigade.

(with some 6 000 men and 160 tanks) formed the spear-head. One brigade stayed behind to guard the Tumpo area against UNITA guerrilla attacks, another formed the garrison of Cuito Cuanavale, and the final two were employed to escort supply convoys on the road between Menongue and Cuito Cuanavale. Facing them was a force of 2 600 men, which would double as the months went by, plus an unknown number of UNITA fighters.

For the SADF, the question was how to respond. Colonel Piet Muller, OC Sector 30 (Okavangoland and western Caprivi), suggested sending in a brigade-sized force west of the Cuito River (see map on p. X) to cut off the FAPLA force, either in the vicinity of Menongue or Cuito Cuanavale itself. The powers that be wanted no part of it, though. Given that the SADF had been able to intervene clandestinely three times already and had gotten clean away with it, they thought they could do it again. Orders coming from Defence and Army Headquarters made it very clear that the intervention would be east of the river, that it had to remain limited and a secret, that no losses whatsoever (either personnel or equipment) could be suffered, and that any success would be ascribed to UNITA.

Militarily, this was madness, but political considerations mostly trump military ones.

And so, a small force – a Valkiri rocket battery, protected by three motorised infantry companies of 32 Battalion – was sent in. The Army's premier conventional unit, 61 Mechanised Battalion Group (61 Mech, as it was generally known) was readied together with air support, just in case. This proved to be insufficient, and on 28 August 61 Mech was released (together with Air Force support) for offensive utilisation.

61 Mech was one of the SADF's interesting innovations. It was a mixed-arms unit, consisting of two mechanised infantry companies with the ubiquitous Ratel-20, an armoured car squadron (Ratel-90), a support company (mobile mortars, an anti-tank platoon, etc.), two artillery batteries (G-5) and a tank squadron (Olifant Mk 1). In operations, these were mostly mixed up in balanced combat teams. This meant that mechanised infantry, armoured cars and other support elements were fused together in combined-arms sub-units of company size. In this case, however, one G-5 battery was exchanged for a 120 mm mortar battery, while – most importantly

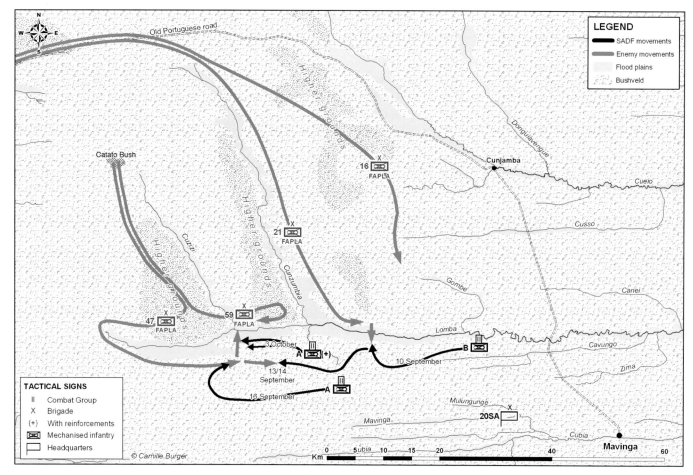

Battles on the Lomba river.

– the Olifant squadron was not activated. (Here we probably see the influence of the fear of escalation!)

Up to 28 August one can understand the SADF command's reticence. Their mind-set, understandably, was influenced by the happenings of 1983, 1985 and 1986. But the release of even the weakened 61 Mech – just under a thousand men with 130 vehicles – and the SAAF was a game-changer. There was simply no way the operation could remain clandestine after this, and therefore, the restrictions made no sense any more. Yet they remained in place.

But there is more. Colonel Muller and other field officers urged headquarters to allow a counteroffensive *west* of the Cuito River. As most of the Angolan force was concentrated on the *eastern* side, Muller's suggestion would result in the South African strength, in accordance with SADF doctrine, being pitted against the enemy's weakest point. But it was turned down, the fear still being that the operation's cover would be blown and that the SADF would become embroiled too deeply in somebody else's fight. Fear of casualties in a country with a white population very sensitive to losing soldiers also played a part.

Nevertheless, the SADF force, now consisting of 61 Mech, plus three 32 Battalion companies and two from 101 Battalion (consisting of indigenous Ovambo troops), plus a G-5 and a 120 mm battery, was organised in a brigade structure – 20 Brigade, with Colonel Deon Ferreira in command. This incremental build-up, ignoring all the lessons of the Savannah debacle, would come back to haunt the South Africans.

Thunderclap on the Lomba

To Ferreira, the tactical situation was worrying. Four brigades, with 6 000 men and 160 tanks, together with overwhelming artillery and air support, were marching southwards. The four formations were grouped two by two together for mutual support – from the west, 47 and 59 brigades, and further east, 16 and 21 brigades. The first named, 47, in fact rounded the source of the Lomba and was already south of it. The others were approaching the northern bank.

On the other side, Ferreira had to juggle his small force in order to block the Angolans. He organised his force in three combat groups, Alpha (most of 61 Mech), Bravo (the elements of 32 and 101 Battalion), and Charlie (a 61 Mech company) as a reserve. They were supported by an understrength artillery regiment as well as a SAAF force of 12 Mirage F1AZ fighter-bombers, 8 Mirage F1CZ fighters, 4 Buccaneer bombers and 3 Canberra bombers. (Of these, the obsolete Canberras were soon discovered to be too vulnerable, and they were quickly packed off home.) And this small force was further hamstrung by Jannie Geldenhuys' order of 7 September, that "[s]afety of own forces and equipment is of cardinal importance and blatant risks may not be taken", and that "operations are to be undertaken as UNITA operations and possible tracing to RSA kept to the minimum".[10]

Ferreira's course of action was clear. He had to prevent 16 and 21 Brigades, closest to Mavinga, from crossing the river. And then he had to keep 47 Brigade, already south of the Lomba to the west, from moving further east and linking up with 59 Brigade on the nearby northern bank.

On 9 September, Commandant Robbie Hartslief, in command of Combat Group Bravo, learnt that 21 Brigade was crossing the river and had already established a bridge-head on the southern shore. The antitank platoon from 32 Battalion immediately engaged the Angolans, together with a 101 Battalion company, but they were too

10 Quoted in Scholtz: *The SADF in the Border War*, pp. 265-266.

weak to dislodge the enemy. Reinforced with another 101 company, and supported by the G-5 artillery battery, Hartslief launched a furious attack the next morning, and the ferocity of the onslaught persuaded the FAPLA infantry to flee in great numbers..

Among Hartslief's weapons were four Ratels equipped with brand-new, still experimental ZT3 anti-tank missiles, and these now experienced their baptism of fire. Some missiles misfired, but others destroyed three tanks, inducing the others to withdraw to the northern side. (Listening to the tapes of the fight, one hears the extatic cries of the South Africans as the missiles destroy the tanks.) The big G-5s took a big toll of the enemy, while the South Africans lost only two wounded. By nightfall the situation was stabilised, and the Angolans' first attempt to cross the Lomba was rebuffed.

Hartslief's force now had the honour to follow their victory up by an attack on 47 Brigade. However, this was a rude awakening. After having ripped into the enemy infantry, the SADF troops came across several counterattacking enemy tanks. Although five tanks were destroyed in exchange for one Ratel (in which, however, four South Africans died), Combat Group Charlie was called in to help. But the enemy was too strong, and Hartslief pulled back. 47 Brigade was not dislodged.

The next attempt on 47 Brigade fell to Commandant Kobus Smit of 61 Mech, who attacked on 16 September. Once again, the fortunes of war did not smile on the South Africans, who were stymied by the incredibly dense bush and could not make headway. After a while, the attack was wisely called off.

On 19 September 21 Brigade tried to cross the river yet again, incredibly at the precise place where the previous attempt was so rudely thwarted. The SADF artillery, however, had their number, the shells bursting in the air above the poor infantry and converting scores of them into mincemeat. The attempt was scotched with severe casualties.

The final battle

So far, FAPLA failed in all its attempts to cross the Lomba and advance to Mavinga. Nevertheless, the fact remained that 47 Brigade was still south of the river, and the formation thus still remained a threat. Therefore, Ferreira ordered Combat Groups Alpha and Charlie (in other words, the entire 61 Mech) to take the formation out.

On 3 October, the final battle of this phase of Operation Moduler unfolded. Under the command of Commandant Kobus Smit, 61 Mech – with Charlie Squadron's Ratel-90s in the van – charged the enemy next to the river. The result was a carnage. Many Angolans fled in panic, and the river turned red with the blood of hundreds of dying and wounded men. However, it was not a cake-walk; other elements of the enemy fought back grimly. Several members of 61 Mech later testified that there was no time to be paralysed with fear; their training kicked in and they went through their paces fairly automatically.

One of the Ratel-90 commanders, David Mannall, later wrote:

The fear I had felt on the approach suddenly melted sway. The only way out this while still alive was to press forward – into the mechanised maelstrom. I was absolutely, coldly, prepeared to unleash the most ruthlessly violent intensity of fire imaginable – anything to subdue and repel the the enemy before he had the opportunity to do the same to me. …It was more open, more intense and violent than anything I had previously encountered. This was the sort of large-scale battle Hollywood seeks, but mostly fails, to emulate when depicting war. In truth, the only way to prosecute this real-life gangbang was to get fucking brutal

with the FAPLA boys; to that end 32 A[...] was working together in perfect harmony v[...] aiming and destroying numerous soft and [...] appeared.[11]

A problem was that the South Africans enc[...] [...]eral Soviet-built T-54/55 tanks, well protected with thi[...] [...]our and with 100 mm guns which would destroy a Ratel with the greatest ease from a distance. The Ratel's armour was thin, designed only to keep out small-arms fire. The armoured car version, with which Charlie Squadron took the brunt of the fighting, was equipped with a low-velocity 90 mm gun, originally designed by the French for their light Panhard armoured car and later put on the Ratel. This gun had the greatest difficulty in penetrating the Angolan tanks' heavy armour. Luckily, due to the thick bush, the distances were very close (sometimes 30-50 metres). Besides, the South Africans had developed a tactic called a fire-belt action, where all – or several – Ratels would fire together at a single target or in the same direction. Mostly, when hit by several 90 mm armour-piercing shells together, the tanks were destroyed. But it took iron nerve to see shell after shell bouncing off the enemy tank and continue firing calmly. The sharp bark of the Ratel-90s were augmented by the staccato stutter of the quick-firing Ratel-20 guns, which caused devastation among the poorly protected Angolan infantry and thinner-skinned vehicles.

Captain. Herman Mulder, 61 Mech's intelligence officer, cooped up in a Ratel-Command vehicle, remembered:

I have never experienced anything like it. I said goodbye to my life at least six times that day. All the time there was bombing and bombing and bombing. The noise was beyond belief. It was driving me mad. All the time I was just thinking: 'I just want to get out of this fucking vehicle.' … I was afraid in the biggest sense you can think of. You know all the time that the next shell might be for you.[12]

As the Ratel guns periodically needed re-adjustment and their ammunition ran out, 61 Mech had to pull back twice to regroup and replenish. With their third charge, the remaining enemy finally broke and by 17h00 the survivors ran for their lives. A full 600 men were killed, effectively destroying 47 Brigade as a functioning formation. The SADF suffered one killed and one Ratel destroyed, although many 61 Mech troops emerged psychologically scarred by the vicious battle. Nevertheless, it was a stunning victory. In addition, the South Africans captured an ultramodern Soviet SA-8 anti-aircraft missile system, which elicited considerable interest from Western intelligence services.

After this battle, FAPLA slowly started withdrawing northwards. Their offensive had failed, having suffered the loss of 61 tanks, 53 BTR-60 armoured personnel carriers, 7 BMP-1 infantry fighting vehicles, 23 BRDM-2 reconaissance patrol vehicles, 20 BM-21 rocker launchers, 1 059 men killed and 2 118 wounded. Tactically, it was an awesome success for the South Africans. But, unknown to them, the worst still lay ahead.

---

11 David Mannall: *Battle on the Lomba. The Day a South African Armoured Nattalion shattered Angola's Last mechanised Offensive. A Crew Commander's Account* (Solihull, Helion, 2014), pp. 168-171.

12 Fred Bridgland: *The War for Africa. Twelve Months that Transformed a Continent* (Gibraltar. Ashanti, 1990), p. 139.

CHAPTER 3
COUNTEROFFENSIVE

Having prevented FAPLA from crossing the Lomba and marching on Mavinga and Jamba, the SADF had by now in fact already done what it set out to do. UNITA was, at any rate for the time being, preserved as a military factor and could continue acting as a bulwark against SWAPO infiltration into Kavangoland and Caprivi. Now the South Africans had to decide on the future. The recent past, however, showed that FAPLA would probably recover, be rearmed with new Soviet weapons and repeat the whole exercise again in 1988. The South Africans understandably wanted this to stop and not be asked to pull UNITA's chestnuts out of the fire every year.

Therefore, on 29 September – even before the final Lomba battle of 3 October – a conference was held at Deon Ferreira's 20 Brigade headquarters near Mavinga. Among those present were President PW Botha, Defence Minister Magnus Malan and his deputy, Wynand Breytenbach, as well as Generals Geldenhuys, Liebenberg and Willie Meyer, and Vice Admiral Dries Putter, Chief of Staff: Military Intelligence.

SADF replanning

The importance of this conference cannot be overstated. After having been briefed on the strategic and operational situation, Botha authorised a new phase in the operation. His strategic instruction was to commence a counteroffensive in order to hit FAPLA so hard that they would not be able to repeat their yearly offensive before the end of 1988. He authorised whatever reinforcements Geldenhuys thought necessary, including, at last, tanks. However, Geldenhuys did not exploit this political backing fully and called in only a modest additional force in the form of 61 Mech's sister mechanised unit, 4 SAI, with a single Olifant tank squadron, as well as more artillery. Seemingly, he still was of the opinion that more forces than those would cause the conflict to be escalated beyond what he thought would be prudent. As Roland de Vries wrote in his memoirs,

> South African forces were inserted piecemeal into the battle. In this way the neglect of a fundamental principle of warfare, namely the *concentration of forces*, plagued the SADF throughout the campaign. The outcome was that a few South African soldiers fought desperately in the frontline for life and death with minimal equipment and logistics against this numerically superior power.[13]

But, like the decision on 18 August to release 61 Mech and the SAAF, this was, in fact, an important game-changer. It raised the political and military stakes considerably, Geldenhuys' reticence notwithstanding.

In order to translate Botha's strategic order onto the operational level, Geldenhuys organised another conference at Rundu, just south of the border in Namibia. Several frontline officers, notably Colonel Roland de Vries and other members of the mechanised mobile warfare brotherhood, argued for the counteroffensive to take place *west* of the Cuito River. (Had that proposal been adopted, De Vries would command the offensive in the west, while Deon Ferreira would be in charge of a holding force in the east. In fact,

A South African tank recovery vehicle. At several times, South African Olifant tanks' tracks were damaged, immobilising them. Tank recovery vehicles like this one were then called in.

The same tank recovery vehicle, photographed from the front. They also doubled as front end loaders, as is happening here.

Liebenberg had already sounded him out on the possibility.) After all, east of the river, the South Africans would come up against at least five enemy brigades. The western approach was guarded by exactly one company, part of the brigade-sized garrison of Cuito Cuanavale. The principles of operational art clearly state that the enemy has to be taken on where he is *weak*, not where he is strong. De Vries' comment was: "At a glance, contemplating the enemy's defence, it was clear that they never truly considered an attack from the west, which was astounding."[14] Therefore, operationally, the course seemed clear, but Geldenhuys was still seemingly driven by the need to keep the war limited.

To be fair, one has, of course, to understand South Africa's broad strategic situation at this juncture. The Government was already in considerable trouble back home with a full-blown revolt in the black townships, led by the ANC. Against this background, an all-out war which would pit South Africa against the full might of the

13 Roland de Vries: *Eye of the Firestorm. Strength lies in Mobility* (Tyger Valley, Naledi, 2013), p. 636.

14 Ibid., p. 652.

SADF Olifant Mk. 1 tanks on the move in the bush early in their deployment. Note the sideplates still in their place. As these plates tended to cause clogging with earth and mud, they were removed later on.

Olifant tanks in the Angolan bush. This photograph gives a fair idea of the kind of terrain they were expected to operate in.

An Olifant tank in an open piece of the bush, with a Ratel in the background. Such open spots were called shonas.

Soviet Union, Cuba and Angola could have only one outcome, a defeat. This obviously had to be avoided. No wonder that there are repeated warnings in SADF documents against South Africa's full involvement beyond what the country was able. But what Geldenhuys, it seems, did not fully grasp, was that Botha's decision had already let the genie out of the bottle. Wars have a nasty way of escalating, and this war was already escalating dangerously. It is difficult to see how de Vries' insistence on advancing west of the Cuito would escalate the war more than what actually happened in any case.

Be that as it may, Geldenhuys decided that an advance west of the river would be too dangerous, and he therefore ordered that it be done east of the river. De Vries and the frontline officers were very frustrated, but orders were orders. (This meant that Ferreira would remain the operational commander, with De Vries as his second in command.) This order, nonetheless, set in a series of events which would directly lead to the SADF's disappointment at Tumpo and Fidel Castro's propaganda victory – a conclusion, obviously, reached with the considerable wisdom of hindsight, but not inaccurate.

The SADF's operational objective
It took some weeks before the reinforcements reached the front, which happened only by month's end. In the meantime there was some desultory fighting between 20 Brigade and the four FAPLA brigades. The ideal would have been to follow up on the Lomba victories immediately and harass the retreating Angolans all the way to Tumpo. But the South Africans were simply too weak for that; they had inadequate operational reserves and had to wait for 4 SAI and the additional artillery. (Here, again, the incremental nature of the SADF's involvement worked against them.) In the meantime, FAPLA worked hard to replace their losses, and by the time the South Africans were ready to start their own offensive, the Angolans were more or less in full strength again.

The South African force was now reorganised. Combat Group Alpha consisted of 61 Mech (minus a mechanised infantry company); Bravo of two motorised infantry companies of 32 and 101 Battalion each plus a 61 Mech mechanised infantry company, and Charlie (4 SAI plus a motorised 32 Battalion company). 20 Brigade became 10 Task Force.

It is important to establish exactly what the South Africans were up to now, as this will provide an important building block for providing an answer later on who won the Battle of Cuito Cuanavale. Many observers, none of whom have bothered to read the actual SADF planning documents and tactical and operational orders, accept as conventional wisdom that the South Africans wanted to capture the town of Cuito Cuanavale. Possession of the town, they say, would provide the springboard for advancing on Menongue and the Angolan Midlands. The end objective would be either the occupation of Luanda itself and the replacement of the MPLA regime with UNITA, or else to split Angola in two. "This was something Pretoria and Savimbi had been aiming at for years," ANC stalwart Ronnie Kasrils asserts, for instance.[15]

This is so vastly exaggerated that it bears no relation to the truth. Reading the original documents, one is struck by the casual references to Cuito Cuanavale. The town figured mainly in the context of an offensive *west* of the Cuito, during which it would have to be taken from behind, from the west. But after the western approach was decided against, all the orders, without exception, stated that FAPLA had to be destroyed *east* of the river, or, alternatively, be driven northwards across the Chambinga river and thence across the Cuito. Then the Cuito's banks had to be mined,

---

15 Ronnie Kasrils: "Turning point at Cuito Cuanavale" (*IOL News*, 23.3.2008, at http://www.iol.co.za/news/world/turning-point-at-cuito-cuanavale-1.393891#. Ve7gtRGqqko).

On the way to attack the Angolans. The Olifant tanks played an invaluable role in the SADF's offensive capacity in Angola.

UNITA had to be empowered to take over the river as a defensive line, after which the South Africans could return home and leave Angola to the Angolans.

To be sure, the orders contain some incidental references in this context to the town. Once, in a document emanating from Kat Liebenberg's office, written towards the end of October, the possible capture of Cuito Cuanavale is mooted if it should prove necessary or convenient. Among the guidelines contained in another document issued in Liebenberg's name, dated 9 December, it is said: "If the opportunity arises to capture Cuito Cuanavale relatively easy, planning should be done to do it."[16] This is the last reference to a possible capture of the town. None of the other planning documents identify the town as an objective. This confirms Geldenhuys' assertion after the war that the capture of Cuito Cuanavale never was an essential part of the SADF objectives.

Ferreira stayed in overall command of the South African brigade, but tasked his new second in command, Colonel Roland de Vries, to design a battle plan. There was no man in the SADF better suited for this. In his book and other publications about mobile warfare, De Vries displayed a thorough understanding of modern mechanised operations. He wrote, inter alia, that the basic purpose of the mobile warfare approach was "to outwit the enemy in an ingenious way, rather than being involved in a head-on full-scale confontation – *Blood is absolutely not the price of victory*" (de Vries' emphasis).[17] In other words, to approach warfare intelligently and rationally, thinking with your head and not with your adrenalin.

The 'Chambinga gallop'

De Vries had made a thorough study of military history, and one battle which caught his attention was Germany's Colonel-General (as he was then) Erwin Rommel's attack on the British Eighth Army in June 1942 in Libya. Rommel had used part of his force to fix the British from the front, but then swung with the main part of his armoured force around their left (southern) flank to attack them from behind. This manoeuvre entered history as the "Gazala Gallop". De Vries now modelled his tactical plan on this, and therefore his own battle became known as the "Chambinga Gallop".

De Vries was especially struck by a remark made by Rommel when reflecting on his desert war campaign in North Africa: "One should endeavour to concentrate one's own forces in space and time, while at the same time seeking to split the opposing forces and to destroy them at different times".[18] He was also heavily influenced by the British military thinker Sir Basil Liddell Hart, who developed the concept of the "indirect approach". In later life, de Vries summarised this approach thus: "Attack with strength against weakness; hit the enemy in his centres of gravity; take the enemy from least expected directions; strike deep and ferociously; threaten his lines of communication, rear areas and command centres".[19]

The walloping FAPLA received at the Lomba notwithstanding, they were still much stronger than the SADF in the area between the Lomba and the Chambinga. De Vries's idea was, therefore, to avoid FAPLA's strength and hit their weak point, the isolated 16 Brigade at the source of the Chambinga. Having trounced 16 Brigade, the

16 Quoted in Scholtz: *The SADF in the Border War*, p. 318.
17 Roland de Vries: *Mobiele Oorlogvoering. 'n Perspektief vir Suider-Afrika*, p. xii.

18 Roland de Vries: *"Mobiele Oorlogvoering – 'n Perspektief vir Suider Afrika" (Mobile Warfare – a Perspective for Southern Africa)*. F.J.N. Harman Uitgewers, Posbus 35226, Menlopark, Pretoria, 0102, 1987, page 52.
19 Roland de Vries: "Mobile warfare the African way – more in the mind and spirit than on paper" (unpublished article, 2015).

Tanks and Ratels moving in concert. This gives a good idea of a SADF mechanised operation, with tanks and mechanised infantry acting in mutual support – a crucial aspect of the SADF's tactics.

This vehicle appears to be a Command Ratel, especially adapted to act as mobile headquarters for a unit or sub-unit. It was armed only with a 12,7 mm machine gun. The crew have hung their clothes on branches, perhaps to dry.

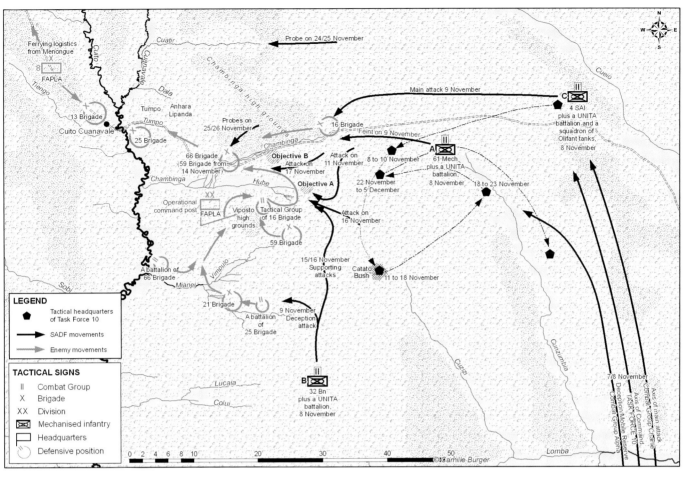

The Chambinga battles.

South Africans would be in an excellent position to cut off the retreat of the other three brigades, still further to the south. As 61 Mech's men, who had been in the field for weeks, were desperately tired and worn down, it was decided that their role would be limited to launching a feint attack on 16 Brigade from the south. When the Angolans' attention was truly fixed in that direction, the fresh 4 SAI would then hit them in their back, from the north.

It was a brilliant plan. However, as the 19th-century Prussian general Helmuth von Moltke once famously said, no battle plan survives first contact with the enemy. Perhaps he exaggerated a bit, but not much. Events conspired to bring about a rather frustrating result for the South Africans.

Nevertheless, things started auspiciously early on the morning of 9 November, when Combat Group Alpha launched its diversionary attack, according to plan. Somewhat later, Charlie weighed in from the other side. The Angolans reacted quickly, launching a counterattack with a tank tactical force. A few minutes later the Olifant squadron, commanded by the very able Major André Retief, swung into action for the first South African tank battle since 1945. Some way southwards, Ferreira, De Vries and the other headquarters staff listened on the radio to Retief's calm orders, so calm that it sounded like a dull exercise, instead of the excited shouts one would expect from men with andrenalin pumping through them.

The Olifants, aided by Ratel-20s and G-5 fire from afar, soon shot out two enemy tanks and trampled the opposing infantry underfoot. The advance went on, and amid the confusion a Ratel-20 even shot out a T-55 with a torrent of armour-piercing rounds (although it was itself destroyed just moments afterwards). Another Angolan counterattack with tanks was stopped in its tracks, and by mid-day the enemy was fleeing with considerable loss of life and equipment.

A South African trooper, with 4 SAI's anti-aircraft guns, saw the battlefield after the event:

The destruction was everywhere around us. The noise, the dust and the smell of death was everywhere. For the first time in my life I saw dead bodies. A head lay on the ground, totally shot off its body, and a body lay half-way out of a ditch. The stink of death was overwhelming. Flies immediately began congregating around the bodies. It was war, and even so, we didn't feel anything any more. We just had to go on.[20]

Charlie's orders were now to exploit its advance to a point opposite the source of the Hube river (see map on page XX) in order to create the killing ground SADF doctrine saw as the tactical ideal. The decisive moment was there. But … anticlimax: Instead of cutting off the retreating enemy, the CO of Combat Group Charlie pulled back his troops to regroup and resupply. His ammunition was low, he later explained, and he was also worried about a FAPLA tactical group of tanks just across the river. Whatever the case, the enemy escaped.

This was a decisive moment. As de Vries explained years afterwards: "After the enemy has been disrupted and defeated, success must be exploited at lightning speed and mercilessly so to keep up the pressure. The enemy must not be given the opportunity to reorganise or regain his wits."[21] Unfortunately – from a South African perspective – this is exactly what happened. Ferreira was livid, but that was that.

20 Rob Jefferies: "Lugafweerbrokkies", in Geldenhuys (ed.): *Ons was Daar*, pp. 270-271.
21 Personal communication from Roland de Vries.

This is how it looks when an enemy cannon round penetrates a SADF Ratel.

This appears to be a hole caused by a Cuban ZSU-23 anti-aircraft cannon (23 mm) in the side of a South African Ratel during Operation Excite in 1988. The Ratel's armour was thin, designed only to withstand small-arms fire.

He and De Vries now decided to have another go two days later This time Alpha would feint from the north and Charlie attack from the south.

Once again, complete success eluded the South Africans. The speed of their attack was considerably slowed down by the unbelievably dense bush, while an Angolan air attack did not exactly help either. They then ran into an Angolan ambush and clashed head-on with a strong FAPLA force. But Major André Retief, in command of the tanks, stayed calm and ordered a fire-belt action (where every vehicle shoots with everything they have in the same direction). This overwhelming firepower did the trick. Another clash ensued, and once again the Angolans could not stand against the South Africans' ferocity. They pulled back again. Another decisive moment approached – and it passed again. Charlie's CO, once again to Ferreira's extreme chagrin, called off the attack to replenish.

But it was not over yet. In the following days, the surviving FAPLA forces further south had to negotiate two rivers, the Vimpulo and the Hube, before reaching the bridge over the Chambinga and safety. For the South Africans, everything went wrong. Their troops positioned themselves wrongly in the dense bush (something which, in those circumstances could happen very easily), and FAPLA proved that it could move surpisingly rapidly in retreat. While the retreating enemy was severely mauled, by 17 November they got clean away to fight another day.

This was almost the end of Ops Moduler. The National Servicemen were due to be demobilised, and new troops had to take their place. There was one final attack on 25 November on the high ground north of the Chambinga, in the perhaps naïve hope that this would be the final push before FAPLA broke completely down. According to some sources, the South African infantry were expected by Kat Liebenberg to attack on foot in bush so thick that even the tanks had trouble moving through it. The infantry would have to attack a strong enemy in well-prepared defences on foot. It elicited angry responses from the field officers, who almost mutinied. Major Dawid Lotter, CO of B Company, 61 Mech, later called it "a suicide mission. The whole concept was against all logic." He tried to convince his new commander, Commandant Mike Muller, but to no avail. "Risking my career, I informed him that, should he insist on the attack being executed, he himself must inform the infantry about this lunacy, and the unacceptable risks involved." Others called the plan "fundamentally stupid".[22] In the end the attack was a damp squib. It never got underway to any extent.

On the face of it, this part of the campaign was a great success. In all instances, the South Africans gave their Angolan counterparts a severe beating. The statistics bear it out: FAPLA lost 34 tanks and about 600 men killed, compared to the 2 Ratels and 16 men on the SADF's side. In fact, the Angolans were getting very demoralised. As Soviet Lieutenant-Colonel Igor Zhdarkin recorded in his diary:

Something quite incomprehensible is happening now: the Angolan troops are almost completely demoralized; the brigades are on average at 45% strength. For every 10-15 shells launched by the enemy, Angolans are able to send only one, if even that much; our reconnaissance operates poorly; and our enemy knows everything about us. The Angolans fear the South Africans like fire and if they hear that 'Buffalo' [32 Battalion] is part of an attack, they throw away all their equipment in panic and flee.[23]

But in warfare, statistics seldom give the full picture. The fact is that, in spite of de Vries' brilliant plans, FAPLA was allowed to get away, albeit not unscathed. Also, the last attack, the one north of the Chambinga which almost caused a mutiny, showed a worrying inability by the SADF high command to think out of the box. As Roland de Vries put it:

The war now started feeling to me like a creeping barrage, similar to what was probably experienced when the front on the Somme became bogged down during World War One. What I feared quietly was that if we did not do something soon to wrest the initiative and mobility back from the tightening noose, we would inevitably be drawn into an attrition trap at Cuito. We were gradually allowing ourselves to be hauled into a funnel. … I mentioned my apprehension to the high-ups a few times. Eventually I realised I had to shut up if I was still interested in further promotion.[24]

22 Dawid Lotter: *61 Mechanised Battalion Group, Bravo Company plus Antitank Platoon, 1987*, pp. 146-147; Fred Bridgeland: *The War for Africa*, p. 230.
23 Zhdarkin: "Cuito Cuanavale: Notes from the Trenches", diary entrance of 11.11.1987, in Shubin and Tokarev (eds.): *Bush War*, p. 57.
24 Quoted in Scholtz: *The SADF in the Border War*, p. 307..

South African tanks mass before moving up to Angola in 1988. No more than two squadrons (24 tanks) were utilised at a time.

Colonel Jan Breytenbach, never known for his tact, opined that the CO of 4 SAI actually had to be fired on the spot.[25] But there was a more fundamental reason for the fact that the South Africans could not completely destroy the four FAPLA brigades. In any battle or campaign, things will go wrong, sometimes horribly so. This virtual certainty may be taken care of by two measures. Firstly, a culture of independent decision-taking on lower command levels. In other words, officers and NCOs should be trained to think on their feet in order to meet unexpected situations. Secondly, any force should

25 Breytenbach: *The Buffalo Soldiers*, p. 285.

have adequate reserves so that these unplanned for setbacks may be countered.

The SADF's training more than adequately met the first requirement. As to the second, it was woefully deficient. With only two mechanised units plus a motorised infantry battalion-sized formation and an artillery regiment, there was no way in which unexpected situations like the above could adequately be met. This was the primary reason why FAPLA got away to fight another day. And that was a direct consequence of the decision to reinforce the original 20 Brigade only with extra artillery, one mechanised battalion group and a single tank squadron.

CHAPTER 4
STORMCLOUDS ARISE

Having driven the enemy northwards back from the Lomba over the Chambinga, geography now changed the tactical nature of the campaign. While the South Africans were fighting south of the Lomba and between the two rivers, there was enough space for them to practise their preferred type of mobile warfare and to be onorthodox, especially when it was led by men of the calibre of Deon Ferreira and Roland de Vries.

However, north of the Chambinga, circumstances were different. The new battleground was hemmed in between the Chambinga in the south, the Cuito in the west and the Cuatir in the north.

This enabled FAPLA to organise their defence in one continuous line. The South Africans now had to assault well prepared, strong defensive lines in full-frontal attacks. Henceforth, attritional warfare would replace mobile warfare – exactly the sort of thing De Vries warned against. It was something the SADF, with its limited resources, could not do for any length of time. This was the direct result of the SADF commanders's earlier decision not to go around FAPLA's flank and direct their attack west of the Cuito river where the Angolans were weak and didn't expect it, but rather to go by the book and attack FAPLA east of the river where they were strongest.

South African officers pause during an orders group. Note the beards. They were given permission to forego shaving, as water was at a premium. Within a short time, they looked rather like their bearded Boer forerunners during the Anglo-Boer War of 1899-1902.

Time for a beer and a Coke in the searingly hot Angolan bush. Even though neither the beer nor the Coke was cold, they were still welcome to those receiving them.

To make things worse, De Vries was ordered to Voortrekkerhoogte to become OC of the Army College. Ferreira's tour of duty was also up. He was replaced by the equally able Colonel Paul Fouché, a veteran of several previous cross-border campaigns and widely respected by his peers. Other unit commanders were rotated as well – Leon Marais (4 SAI) was replaced by the dynamic Jan Malan, while Mike Muller had already taken the place of Kobus Smit as OC 61 Mech, and was now in turn replaced with Koos Liebenberg (all Commandants, or Lieutenant-Colonels). Jean Lausberg remained in command of the all-important artillery.

Reorganisation

The abortive attack of 25 November was Operation Moduler's last gasp. The conscript troops' time was up. They departed for home base in South Africa to be demobilised and returned to civilian life, wondering how their contribution would be received back home. One of the new troops coming in to replace the old ones at 61 Mech got a huge fright when he saw those on their way home:

[W]e were greeted by a phalanx of the wildest, dirtiest-looking people I had ever seen. These guys had not shaved for months, and it looked as though they had not been near water for long. They were wearing filthy overalls and their hair was long. They clapped and cheered as we walked through their ranks to our 'new' Ratel. I thought to myself, 'These guys look like animals, what the hell have they been doing up there?' As for the Ratel, there was no doubt that it had been through some serious shit over the past few months. It was pretty battered and quite a few things needed fixing before we could even think about taking it into a combat situation.[26]

New troops and reinforcements arrived to take their place in what would now be called Operation Hooper. An additional tank squadron, manned by Citizen Force troops from Regiment Pretoria, appeared at the front (after six weeks these would be replaced with a squadron from Regiment Malopo). 32 Battalion was pulled out for a clandestine operation west of the Cuito to cut the enemy's supply lines, an operation which was, however, conducted with insufficient force and vigour to make a significant impact. This

was the generals' only concession to the repeated pressure from the frontline to switch the operation's spearpoint to the west of the Cuito. Within a few weeks the unit would be back on the "eastern" front. Being a motorised infantry unit, it would subsequently only play a supporting role in a war that would become increasingly tank-heavy. The brunt fell squarely on the men of 61 Mech, 4 SAI and the tank squadrons, an indication of how intensive the operations now became. Which makes it all the more incomprehensible why the campaign was conducted with such woefully insufficient forces, something which afterwards elicited angry feelings from frontline officers and troops.

It also begs the question why the SADF high command did not order more tanks to the front. Even President P.W. Botha asked during his visit to the front on 29 September why there were no tanks present at that stage, indicating that there would be political backing for it. Once again, the fear of escalation would seem the only explanation – perhaps understandable, but unwise from a military point of view.

On the "other side of the hill", FAPLA – by this time clearly advised by Cubans – organised an intelligent defence in depth. Their flanks rested on the Cuatir in the north and the Chambinga in the south, with the result that they could not be outflanked any more. In fact, three defence lines, one behind the other, were established in considerable depth. The first was a few kilometres from the river; the second nearer to it, while the third was positioned just east of the stream.

Even for a strong force, it would be a devilishly difficult task to carry out the original SADF operational order, still valid, namely to drive FAPLA back over the river. Let alone for an understrength brigade of two mechanised battalion groups with just two tank squadrons, two armoured car squadrons and an artillery regiment. This allowed the South Africans no reserves, contradicting a fundamental rule of warfare. One is rather surprised at the lack of understanding of modern conventional warfare at SADF and Army Headquarters, but the generals' expectation was that it would take only one final push for the entire FAPLA edifice to collapse. Famous last words: FAPLA admittedly was not the world's best army, far from it, but they now at last had intelligent (Cuban) leadership, and their defence was made much easier by the help they received from the terrain, which strongly favoured the defence.

---

26 Clive Holt: *At thy Call we did not Falter. A Frontline Account of the 1988 Angolan War, as Seen Through the Eyes of a Conscripted Soldier* (Cape Town, Zebra, 2005), p. 32.

The troops often threw their *ratpacks* (ration packs) together to brew a kind of stew. Anything to break the monotony of the *ratpacks*.

A tank recovery vehicle digging trenches.

The man in the camouflage uniform in the background appears to be a FAPLA prisoner of war.

The SADF forges ahead

It would take about five weeks before the SADF was able to do battle again. The newcomers had to get accustomed to the difficult conditions. That included the incredible energy-sapping, humid heat, the millions of flies which drove the soldiers crazy, a badly overburdened logistic apparatus and resulting shortage of just about everything, from toilet paper to socks and weapons systems' spare parts. Especially the artillery and tanks had to contend with growing unserviceability as time went on. As a result, the troops' morale started suffering.

In addition, the SADF now started deviating from its own doctrine in another crucial aspect. When Paul Fouché presented a battle plan for his first attack on the outer FAPLA defence line, Jannie Geldenhuys vetoed it as being "too aggressive" and risking too many casualties. (It was, in fact, an excellent, well-considered plan.) From here on the generals would breathe ever more down the frontline officers' necks and make things very difficult for them. Reading their accounts after the war, a considerable anger comes through about this meddling. It was contrary to SADF doctrine, according to which the high command would set out the objectives, leave the tactical commanders to do their thing and only intervene if these stepped outside the allowed parameters. But there was nothing the frontline officers could do but swallow it; orders were, after all, meant to be obeyed. Until the end of the war, this almost became

a standard practice and would be responsible for many unnecessary problems.

However one looks at it, the plan decided on instead appears pretty naïve. To begin with, it was thought that FAPLA could simply be intimidated into a retreat by an artillery barrage. If this did not happen, UNITA infantry would attack with SADF fire support. Only if UNITA could not succeed, would 61 Mech and 4 SAI get involved.

The bombardment duly took place on 2 January 1988. But of course, the FAPLA soldiers, secure in their strong defensive positions, did not run away. And the attack by UNITA, not organised, equipped and trained for high-intensity conventional warfare, was squarely repulsed. And so, on 13 January the SADF was forced to weigh in after all.

In spite of the cunning way in which the defences were organised, this attack was a success. While some defenders fought bravely and pulled back in an organised fashion, others ran away in panic. Enemy air attacks were wide off the mark and had very little influence. At one stage, the bemused South Africans watched about 30 stark naked Angolans stampeding past, running for their lives. The fighting was hard and lasted until well after dark, and a big hole was punched in the outer FAPLA defence line. Jan Malan found himself breaking through with the bridge over the Cuito within his reach. But he had only four serviceable tanks left, and as there were

On the outside this T-54/55 looks undamaged, but it was in fact destroyed by an Olifant during the attack on 16 Brigade on 9 November 1987.

no reserves – the perennial SADF problem – Fouché had no option but to call him back.

According to orders, the captured positions were now turned over to UNITA. However, when fresh FAPLA troops launched a fierce counterattack a day or two later, UNITA folded and withdrew, as the frontline SADF officers knew they would. The positions the South Africans had fought so hard for were once again in enemy hands. Which meant that the 13 January attack was all in vain. Major-General Willie Meyer, GOC SWA, lamely explained to the troops that it was sometimes desirably to let the enemy retake a position so that it could be destroyed in a later attack. Not suprisingly, the men were not greatly impressed with him or his message.

Ominously, signs were now picked up of Cuban troops among the defenders. Indeed, Cuban dictator Fidel Castro had felt that the South African advance forced him to respond. We will look at his strategy later; suffice it for the time being to say that he wanted to elevate the defence of Cuito Cuanavale to a grand heroic battle between good and evil. A tank tactical group, equivalent to a squadron, was sent post-haste to the front to stiffen the defenders' spines.

It took until 14 February before the attempt could be repeated, this time under the command of Colonel Pat McLoughlin, who took over from Paul Fouché (Fouché was sent home to mobilise a Citizen Force brigade). The attack started quite well, the enemy suffering considerable losses. But then the Cubans made their presence felt by organising an ambush just inside the treeline at the edge of a shona, an open clearing in the bush. To the South Africans' surprise, the Cuban tanks carried out a furious counterattack there. But although these, under the command of Lieutenant-Colonel "Ciro" Gómez Betancourt, were described as very aggressive and death-defying by their South African counterparts, they were not handled

well and attacked all bunched up (no doubt due to their tactical inexperience). All but one tank, that of the brave commander, were knocked out. At the same time, a Ratel-20 was shot out with four dead. Although this was another SADF tactical victory, the Cuban counterattack won time and prevented the South Africans from breaking through to the river. A desultory FAPLA counterattack was launched during the night to retake the lost positions, but was rather easily repulsed.

With this, the easternmost Angolan defence line crumbled, and they had to fall back to the second one.

The fighting since the beginning of the year proved to be disastrous for the enemy in terms of men and equipment lost. Together FAPLA and the Cubans had 532 men killed and 27 tanks destroyed or captured, compared to the 4 deaths on the South African side and 1 Ratel destroyed. The South Africans could show something for this, because the outer FAPLA defence line was pierced, and the Angolans retained only a toe-hold on the eastern banks of the Cuito.

But this was the nadir of the South African advance. They still had not succeeded in driving the Angolans completely over the river, and it was no problem for the Angolans to replace their losses In addition, the SADF's succcssion of victorics would now end.

South Africans relaxing in front of their Ratel Judging by the number on the side, this Ratel belongs to the supply echelon.

South African medics relaxing in the field. These personnel sometimes had to treat most horrific sounds. Often they saved their comrades' lives; sometimes they could not.

A Kwêvoël logistical vehicle, apparently carrying a fuel bladder on the back.

CHAPTER 5
INTO THE CAULDRON

Up to now, the SADF had experienced an uninterrupted series of tactical victories, even though these victories, for several reasons, did not all translate into operational success. Presently, the South Africans would have to experience the bitter taste of tactical defeat. We shall analyse the outcome of the campaign as a whole on balance later on.

We have seen that the open, wide spaces of the battlefield south of the Chambinga had been replaced by the rather limited room for manoeuvre north of that river, and that the South Africans were forced into direct, frontal attacks on well-prepared Angolan defensive positions. This was the direct result of the SADF generals' decision to avoid the open spaces west of the Cuito River and to attack the bulk of the enemy forces east of the river. Whereas their capacity to manoeuvre – the South Africans' forté – was, therefore, diminished, it would be completely eliminated in this final stage of the battle which now lay ahead.

The Cubans had by this time taken over the tactical command of the front in the vicinity of Cuito Cuanavale. Even more importantly, Cuban dictator Fidel Castro esconced himself in a big bunker in Havana, Cuba's capital, and directed the battle from there. One may undoubtedly conduct a legitimate political debate about Castro's

Communist ideology and his credentials as a liberation fighter. What his actions make certain, however, is that he had a cunning military mind and considerable tactical and strategic acumen. He would now get ample opportunity to prove it.

Preparations

Castro and his field commanders on the scene clearly made a thorough tactical evaluation of the fighting up to now. Unfortunately, one is not privy to all their inner thoughts, as very few sources about their tactical thinking and planning are available. Nevertheless, judging by their actions in the next few weeks, one may deduce that they, quite correctly, came to the conclusion that FAPLA simply could not stand against a determined SADF attack, even when strongly dug in and fortified. In fact, throughout the entire Border War, FAPLA always folded against a SADF assault, even if the South Africans at times had to exert themselves considerably. So, the conclusion seems to have been that the SADF had to be *prevented* from making contact with the FAPLA defenders in the first place. And this would be done through a combination of cunningly placed minefields, artillery barrages and air attacks.

They were further aided by geography, which greatly favoured

Another view of a tank recovery vehicle.

the defence.

Firstly, the South Africans were on the end of a long logistical umbilical line, starting in Pretoria and Cape Town, winding its way over thousands of kilometres to Grootfontein in the north of SWA. From there the supplies were flown by Air Force transports to Mavinga, after which lorries had to "bundu-bash" (in SADF parlance) to the front. With too few lorry drivers, as well as a logistical apparatus not suited for these circumstances, the frontline troops had to make do with a perennial shortage of just about everything. This meant that a considerable percentage of the South Africans' main weapons systems – tanks, armoured vehicles, artillery pieces – were always unserviceable. Through superhuman efforts the techicians, known as "tiffies" in the SADF (short for *artificers*), succeeded in ensuring that most systems were available when the chips were down, but at times it really was touch and go.

On the other side, the enemy's supplies came by ship to the harbour town of Namibe, and from there by rail to Menongue. From Menongue, convoys snaked down the road to Cuito Cuanavale. And, although Unita guerrilla attacks and SAAF air strikes sometimes caused horrendous casualties and destruction, this was never enough to disrupt the enemy's operations decisively.

In addition, the western bank of the Cuito river (in Angolan/ Cuban hands) was decidedly higher than the western side, where the South Africans were positioned. Which meant that their artillery could range far and wide and hamper the South African attacks once these got rolling.

Geography also favoured the enemy in the air war. But we shall look at that somewhat later.

In the meantime, the Angolans and Cubans took time to fortify themselves properly with trenches, bunkers and minefields, all

Tank crews enjoying a beer. The supply echelon frequently succeeded in transporting beer to the front in order to keep up the morale of the troops.

covered by some 80 artillery pieces – guns and rocket launchers. A South African trooper who took part in the forthcoming battles, described the battlefield as seen from his side:

The positions around Tumpo were now heavily fortified, with FAPLA even clearing large areas of bush so they would be able to see the South African advance and get a clear shot at us as we came in to attack them. They had also laid extensive minefields in front of their positions to stop any advancing force. ... They had also taken all of their damaged tanks and dug them in as an additional line of defence. These tanks could not be driven or

The SWAWEK dam in 1988

move out to meet the advancing force, but their weapons systems were still fully functional, so by digging them into the ground, they could take aim at leisure and pick us off as we advanced. All that could be seen of the tanks were the turrets and barrels making them a more difficult target to acquire and destroy. The odds were heavily stacked against us for taking Tumpo and the Cuito Bridge, but we were going to give it our best shot.[27]

Three SADF attacks would now follow in an attempt to occupy the last FAPLA bridgehead on the eastern side of the Cuito, also known as the Tumpo triangle. Possession of this piece of real estate was important to both sides. If the Angolans and Cubans lost Tumpo, the last stumbling block to prevent the SADF from taking Cuito Cuanavale would fall. And, although the village itself had little tactical or operational value, Fidel Castro had elevated its defence to a symbol of defiance against a mighty, but perfidious enemy. Cuito Cuanavale would not fall, he decreed from his bunker in Havana, come what may.

On 20 February he cabled his military commander in Angola, *General de Division* (Major-General) Arnaldo Ochoa Sanchez (who, by the way, was later sentenced to death on probably trumped-up charges of smuggling), that it would be a "total disaster" if the South Africans broke through to the Cuito: "Should that happen, it would be hard to hold Cuito [Cuanavale] and the political and moral consequences for FAPLA and the Angolan government would be terrible." On the 21st he continued:

What would happen if tomorrow the enemy breaks through the

An Olifant tank in the bush. Note that its 105 mm gun is turned backwards in order to minimise the danger of being damaged. It indicates that no danger is imminent.

line with a powerful attack in the direction of the river? ... we feel there is a lack of foresight, that those in charge there don't realize the terrible effects on the military and political situation and on morale a disaster with the forces east of the river would have, and we don't even have a few boats to do what the British did with theirs in Dunkirk.[28]

Of course, as the original SADF documents in the archives

---

27 Holt: *At thy Call we did not Falter*, pp. 84-85.

28 *Case 1/1989* (Havana, José Martti, 1989), testimony by Fidel Castro, 12.7.1989, p. 387-388.

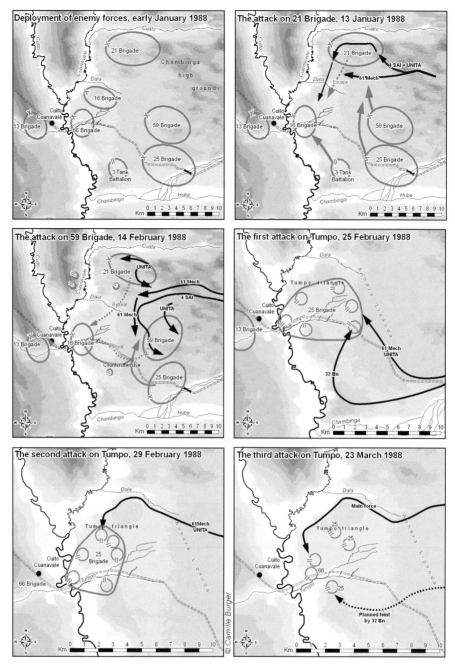

Tumpo.

show, the South Africans' interest in the village was desultory. They had no real plans to occupy the town, let alone to push through to Menongue and the Angolan Midlands or even to Luanda. But, of course, Castro could not know this; one suspects that he really believed that Cuito Cuanavale was the South African target. In reality, all the written SADF operational and tactical orders make it clear that the attackers would not advance further than the eastern bank of the Cuito river.

Nevertheless, Castro's understandable misreading of the South African intentions notwithstanding, his orders to the field commanders on the spot show considerable military understanding on his part. For instance, he saw that the forward defence lines would not hold against the South Africans. He therefore ordered a pull-back in order to shorten – and thus strengthen – them. This move was forestalled by the South African breakthrough of 14 February, which forced the Angolans and Cubans to do what Castro wanted in the first place.

Tumpo 1

On 25 February the South Africans carried out their first attempt to drive the enemy out of the Tumpo bridgehead. Colonel Pat McLoughlin was now in command of the SADF force, which had reverted to the designation of 20 Brigade. Once again, the generals breathed down the frontline officers' necks. McLoughlin's tactical plan had to be approved by Kat Liebenberg and Jannie Geldenhuys, as well as Defence Minister Magnus Malan.

For this attack, 61 Mech (with both tank squadrons) would be in the van, once again under the leadership of Mike Muller. 4 SAI, under Commandant Cassie Schoeman, would be the main reserve. Their assault would be preceded by an advance of 32 Battalion, which would occupy a horseshoe-shaped FAPLA position in the southeast of the battlefield (see map on page XX).

By first light, the men from 32 Battalion stormed their target, but there was no resistance; the enemy had evacuated it in time. This was in accordance with the Cuban commanders' apparent tactics to avoid contact with the South Africans.

But this was the only South African success of the day. The main

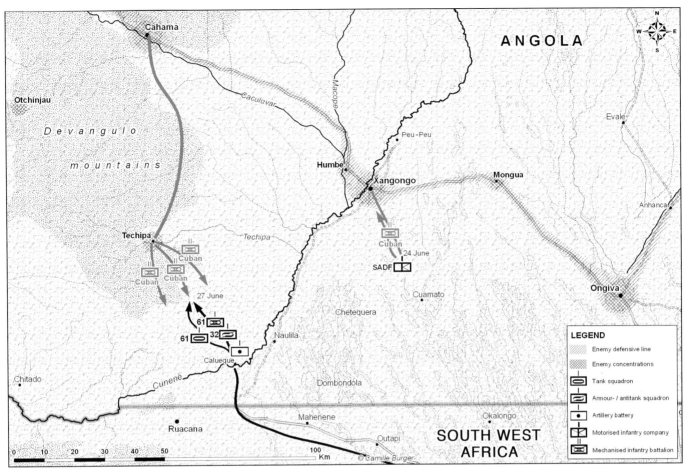

The Cuban advance.

force next advanced northwards just inside the treeline, but then they had to cross an open floodplain, known as the Amhara Lipanda. And there the trouble started. 61 Mech stumbled into a recently laid minefield, which damaged Muller's own tank. The enemy let fly with everything they had, supported by MiG air attacks. These kept the SADF artillery from firing, making Muller's position very precarious.

With considerable effort, a path was cleared through the minefield. But it meant a delay of about three hours, while three tanks were damaged. The force now advanced further under intense fire, and by 15:00, five Ratels having been hit, Muller decided that his force was dead in the water. He stopped the attack and pulled back.

Simply looking at the figures, it was another SADF victory: FAPLA lost 172 men and the Cubans 10, while 6 or 7 tanks were destroyed. Conversely, the South Africans lost 4 killed in action and 10 wounded. Several tanks and Ratels were damaged but repaired, while 3 vehicles were burned out. (Unita's losses are unknown. If these are taken into account, the SADF "victory" might perhaps look less convincingly.)

But it was no SADF victory. It was a defeat. The attacking force got nowhere; Tumpo stayed solidly in FAPLA hands. The only advantage for the South Africans was that the Angolans withdrew the bulk of their forces over the river and kept only a some 800 troops on the eastern side. Given their tactics to avoid contact with their adversary, this did not benefit the attackers very much. Besides, having been in the field for weeks without proper supplies, and suffering from illness, the South African ranks were depleted, while the troops' morale suffered.

Tumpo 2

The inadequate SADF logistical apparatus meant that spare parts for the weapons systems were now at a premium. In fact, only half of the tanks, Ratel-90s and G-5s were serviceable for the second Tumpo attack. McLoughlin nevertheless came up with a cunning plan: He would utilise the SADF's superior night-fighting abilities to launch a night attack, and also draw away the enemy's attack with a 4 SAI feint in the south, exactly the direction whence the first attack came. The main thrust would then commence in the north, led by 61 Mech, again with all the available tanks. The weather forecast for the designated day, 1 March, was cloudy, preventing the enemy from utilising his command of the air.

It failed again. The Cubans apparently were not fooled by the southern feint, and laid a minefield exactly in the path where the main force would advance. In addition, it was raining hard, making a night attack impossible. The attack had to be postponed several hours to first light. But together with the coming of daylight, the clouds lifted – and within a short time, the air was swarming with MiGs, swooping down like angry hornets. And, although the bombing was, as usual, wholly inaccurate (some bombs even exploding on Angolan positions), this did not help at all.

The South Africans advanced in the face of overwhelming enemy fire. Mike Muller, in tactical command of the attack, ordered a fire-belt action, which subdued the enemy reaction somewhat. However, the poor UNITA infantry, who rode unprotected on top of the tanks, suffered horribly. No-one knows how many perished that day, but according to eye-witness accounts, the number was high.

Then the attackers stumbled into a carefully planned killing area, drawing fire from three sides, with anti-tank weapons, D-30

An Olifant tank moving towards the enemy. Note that the sideplates have been removed.

The official caption to this photographs indicates that these men from the School of Armour survived an ambush in Angola in 1988.

An SADF recovery vehicle on a big tank transporter lorry.

A 21 Brigade BM-21 multiple rocket launcher, disabled by an Olifant on 13 January 1988.

An SA-13 anti-aircraft missile vehicle, knocked out by a SADF tank on 14 February 1988. The Angolans suffered heavy losses on this day.

The tank squadron men with 20 SA Brigade had their own mascot, a little monkey, with them.

A 130 mm M-46 gun and an Ural gun tractor, belonging to 21 Brigade, captured in the Angolan bush.

A water tower at Ongongo in the north of SWA during 1988.

An Angolan SA-13 anti-aircraft missile system captured by the SADF on 14 February 1988.

The Angolan bush looks as if it was ploughed over after the big attack of 13 January 1988. The barrel in front belongs to a Browning 7,72 mm machine gun on the turret of either an Olifant or a Ratel.

A UNITA anti-tank squad standing ready to advance. Unita foot soldiers played a subsidiary role to the mechanised forces of the SADF.

A BM-21 multiple rocket launcher system belonging to 21 Brigade, destroyed during March 1988. In the background a Ratel-20 may be seen.

artillery, rockets, the feared 23 mm cannon and machine guns. The intensity of the fire was reminiscent of El Alamein or Stalingrad. And then Muller received a report that enemy tanks were on the move. It later transpired that the report was exaggerated, but this was the last straw. Muller asked permission from McLaughlin, OC 20 Brigade, to break off the attack. But the Commandant's request had to be bounced up right to the Chief of the SADF, Jannie Geldenhuys. This was totally against SADF doctrine, which left tactical commanders with the maximum freedom to make decisions on their own, provided they stay within the parameters of the overall plan. It shows how the campaign was being micromanaged from the top. Nevertheless, permission was granted, and 61 Mech started the withdrawal.

Once again, the SADF was thwarted. For a second time, an intelligent defence prevented them from making contact with FAPLA, and they were stopped in their tracks through a combination of landmines, artillery fire and air attacks. As McLoughlin wrote in his war diary on 1 March, just after the attack: "The enemy is strong and clever."[29]

Tumpo 3

The South African conscripts' time was now up, and it was time for the men of 61 Mech, 4 SAI and the two tank squadrons to return home. Paul Fouché now returned as OC of a new formation, 82 Mechanised Brigade, consisting entirely of Citizen Force

29 Scholtz: *The SADF in the Border War*, p. 350.

A bridge, built by SADF combat engineers, with a Command Ratel leading the convoy. As the guns are turned backwards, no danger is imminent

troops. The SADF was, in fact, running out of soldiers trained for conventional warfare and had to fall back on reservists. The new formation consisted of two mechanised infantry battalions from Regiment De la Rey and Regiment Groot Karoo, two tank squadrons from Regiment President Steyn (with brand new tanks), a Ratel-90 squadron from Regiment Mooi River, and two artillery batteries with the formidable G-5 (155 mm) and the World War II-vintage G-2 (5,5-inch, or 140 mm), a battery of 120 mm mortars (44 Parachute Brigade), and a troop of Valkiri rocket launchers (127 mm) from 19 Rocket Regiment. These were buttressed by elements of 32 Battalion and, of course, an unknown number of lightly-armed UNITA infantry.

This meant that Operation Hooper was finished, and Operation Packer took its place.

Paul Fouché would be assisted by Commandant Gerhard Louw, an experienced, intelligent armour officer, who would command the spearhead of the final attempt to dislodge FAPLA from its last bridgehead east of the Cuito. Louw was rather dissatisfied with the short time he had to organise refresher training for the reservists and to establish the necessary bond of trust between commander and troops. But orders were orders, and when the command came, he had no option but to attack.

Besides, the enemy now got a breather of three weeks to prepare their defences. They laid new mine-fields and dug in 130 mm shells together with their powerful anti-tank mines, ensuring that any tank detonating these devices, would not simply be temporarily immobilised (as in previous attacks), but would actually be destroyed. The Cubans also deliberately left gaps in the mine-fields and trained their anti-tank weapons on them. All in all, it would be tactical madness to conduct a full-frontal attack here with troops

who were, moreover, unready through no fault of their own.

Besides, Fouché and Louw were ordered from above to use the same approach as during Tumpo 2. This was in complete disregard of the tactical dictum never to repeat a failed attack along the same route. Fouché and Louw protested and even enlisted the support of people like General Constand Viljoen (Geldenhuys' predecessor as Chief of the SADF and father of the Army's mobile warfare doctrine) and Brigadier Eddie Webb, Commander of the Army Battle School at Lohatlha. These communicated with Kat Liebenberg, but Liebenberg, having little understanding of modern conventional warfare, stuck to his guns. According to one account he said something like "Why don't you form up the tanks and infantry in an extended line and move forwards, firing until the enemy crosses to the other side of the river?"[30] Which was just about the height of naïveté.

Naïveté or not, orders were orders and meant to be followed. The plan called for a rather desultory feint by 32 Battalion and UNITA in the south, which did not fool the enemy at all.

As could be expected, the attack failed once again. First, only one of the tank rollers which had to detonate mines before they exploded were available. And then, when the enemy artillery opened fire, the inexperienced reservists scattered in panic, and Gerhard Louw had to run around under enemy fire to round them up again. Then the tanks ran into one of the boosted mine-fields, and the only tank fitted with a roller was heavily damaged. A path was cleared with some effort. But when the advance was resumed, they immediately ran into a second minefield. Three tanks were immobilised by the powerful, boosted mines. Louw ordered a fire-belt action and had one tank towed out, but the other two were too heavily damaged

30 Scholtz: The SADF in the Border War, p. 353.

UNITA also had its successes. This BTR-60 infantry fighting vehicle from 21 Brigade was disabled by UNITA troops.

A BRDM-2 armoured car from 21 Brigade, captured by the South Africans.

An Angolan T-55 stand folornly in the middle of nowwhere having been destroyed by the SADF.

and had to be left behind.

The heaviest concentration of fire in any military action since World War II now descended from the barrels of the concentration of enemy guns and rocket launchers on the South Africans. To make things worse, the clouds lifted early in the afternoon, and the enemy fire was augmented by – luckily inaccurate – air attacks. The attack force was as dead as a duck in the water, and it would be madness to continue. By 15:30 Louw ordered a pull-back.

One damaged tank was pulled out, but the other three had to be left behind. Louw requested permission from Fouché to destroy them with artillery fire, but Kat Liebenberg – who was also present – actually forbade it. He said they could be retrieved later. Apparently, it never dawned on him that the enemy was in fact now in possession of the battlefield. And so, three South African Olifant tanks fell into

enemy hands, giving a propaganda coup on a silver platter to Fidel Castro, who had photographs of the tanks disseminated world-wide. This gave credence to the Cuban-Angolan propaganda of a glorious victory over the racist South Africans.

However one looks at it, the hard fact is that the SADF failed in its attempts to drive FAPLA and the Cubans across the Cuito, as their orders stated. That Cuito Cuanavale did not fall, is irrelevant, as the village never really was in their sights.

We shall come back to this when the outcome of the entire campaign is analysed.

Olifant tanks excercising in preparation for the Angolan operation in 1988.

A South African officer addressing UNITA soldiers before an attack. The SADF and UNITA frequently cooperated in tactical attacks.

This Olifant was damaged by an Angolan BM-21 rocket on 25 February 1988.

The crew of a Command Ratel posing in front of their vehicle. Note the 12,7 mm machine gun, which was regarded as far too puny by many of the crews, longing for the heavier punch of the 20 mm or even the 90 mm gun.

The official caption to this photograph indicates that these men are the National Servicemen leader group at the School of Armour in 1988.

Tanks advancing at full speed during an exercise in the Free State in 1988.

The iron bar in front of this tank is meant to facilitate "bundu-bashing" – breaking through bushes without damaging the vehicle

An SADF recovery vehicle on a big tank transporter lorry.

A bridge, built by SADF combat engineers, over the Cuito river, with an Olifant tank crossing it, during Operation Hooper in early 1988.

The area in front has clearly been flattened by artillery. This photograph was taken on 13 January 1988, the date of a major SADF attack.:

Smoke still permeates the battlefield after the battle of 13 January 1988.

A proud South African poses on a damaged Angolan tank, disabled on 14 February 1988.

A captured Soviet Ural truck struggling through the bush. Judging from the barrel in the forefront, the photo was taken from an Olifant tank.

An Olifant tank at Mavinga. Mavinga was a key objective of the Angolan offensive, due to its airstrip.

Twelve South African soldiers died when Cuban MiG-23s attacked the Calueque dam on 26 June, 1988, the last day of the fighting. This was the Buffel armoured personnel carrier alongside which the deceased stood.

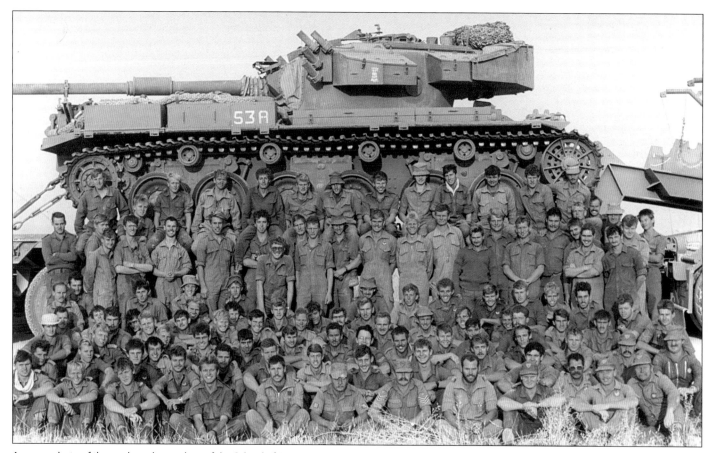

A group photo of the ready tank squadron of the School of Armour, serving with 61 Mechanised Battalion Group in 1988.

This is how a battlefield looks after the battle. These positions were occupied by FAPLA until being captured by the SADF.

CHAPTER 6
END-GAME

The analysis in SADF circles after the failure of the three attacks to drive FAPLA and the Cubans out of their bridge-head at Tumpo, was that it would not be worthwhile to continue. The enemy was too strongly dug in. Besides, South Africa had succeeded in 95% of its operational objectives. After all, the plan was to either destroy the enemy forces east of the Cuito or to drive them over the river, to fortify it as a defence position, enable UNITA to take over and to go home. The enemy only retained a toe-hold east of the river.

Operation Packer was, therefore, followed up by Operation Displace. A small force, designated Combat Group 20, under command of Commandant Piet Nel of 1 Parachute Battalion, was placed in the vicinity of Tumpo with orders to simulate a far bigger formation and keep the enemy guessing. This force, consisting of the anti-tank squadron of 32 Battalion (with Ratel-90s), a motorised infantry company of 101 Battalion, a G-5 and a Valkiri battery and two combat engineer troops, aggressively simulated the continued presence of a brigade until the end of August, when they returned to SWA.

Fidel Castro's strategy

By the end of 1987, Cuban dictator Fidel Castro had serious problems. When he first intervened in Angola on the side of the Marxist MPLA in 1975, he was enthusiastically supported by the Cuban population. It also won him considerable international prestige, especially in the Communist bloc and the Third World.

It is true that Castro was a brutal dictator, not worried by niceties like human rights. But he also had finely attuned political antennae, and he realised that his intervention in Angola should not degenerate into an open-ended participation in somebody else's civil war. Therefore, having ensured the MPLA's victory, by 1977 he started drawing down his military presence in Angola. But the SADF's airborne assault on Cassinga and the land attack on Chetequera in May 1978 convinced him that his job was not yet done, and he reinforced his troops there again.

But, at the same time, Castro also realised that his people's support would not be indefinite. He thus tried to keep his forces in Angola from being placed in harm's way. They were largely restricted to garrison duties, mainly in the vicinity of Luanda, as well as training and advising MPLA troops. They also manned a series of fortified

The Angolans sometimes dug in their tanks. This simply gave the South Africans a static target to shoot at, an opportunity which they grabbed with both hands.

Very little of the fauna and flora survive after a pitched battle.

guard posts along the railway between Namibe and Menongue. Castro viewed these as a kind of trip-wire to prevent the SADF from moving too deep into Angola and even marching on to Luanda in order to replace the MPLA with UNITA. (Of course, although that idea was, at times, entertained in SADF circles, there was enough realism to know that South Africa simply did not have the strength to do that. But, of course, Castro had no way of knowing this.)

By the second half of the eighties, the Cuban population's patience with their military's presence in Angola was wearing thin. In 1987, the Deputy Chief of the Cuban Air Force, Brigadier-General Rafael del Pino, defected to the United States, where he gave a lot of valuable intelligence to the Americans (and, through them, to the South Africans as well). He also gave a series of interviews to Radio Martti, the free Cuban radio station in Miami, Florida, in which he told of the low morale of the Cuban forces in Angola. For instance, he said that "in recent years, Angola has become a place of punishment, or a place to send difficult officers, i.e., first officers or commanders who do not enjoy the trust of their superior commanders or who have morale problems or problems of command and qualification. The choice of Angola as a place of punishment has created great problems."[31]

Angola was "a dead-end street," he said. "Angola – many of us military men have discussed this – is Cuba's Viet Nam. If there is anybody at all who has any faith in victory, it's only Fidel and Raúl Castro [Fidel's younger brother]. I have spoken with officers of my own rank, and among us there is the utter conviction that there is no solution to the case of Angola. It is a lost cause …"[32] No wonder that Castro's newly-appointed field commander in Angola, Major-General Arnaldo Ochoa Sanchez, reportedly complained that "I have been sent to a lost war to take on the burden of defeat."[33]

In addition, the international climate was changing. The American government of President Ronald Reagan was actively aiding UNITA. And a new man took charge in the Kremlin in 1985, President Mikhail Gorbachev, who realised that his country was economically and politically very near to breaking point. Moscow's political will to continue carrying the burden for the notoriously inefficient Cuban economy and its expensive wars in Angola and Ethiopia was winding down.

Castro clearly knew that he was riding down a *cul de sac*. He was

31 : *General Del Pino Speaks. Military Dissension in Castro's Cuba* (n.p., The Cuban-American National Foundation, 1987), p. 12.

32 Ibid., p. 17.

33 *Case 1/1989*, p. 51, testimony by Raúl Castro, 26.6.1989.

This BRDM-2 armoured car of 21 Brigade did not survive.

The number on the side of this Olifant tank indicates that it belongs to the ready squadron from the School of Armour, Troop 1, and commanded by the troop sergeant.

The tank of the tank squadron's commander moves past a captured 130 mm M-46 artillery piece.

Immediately they stopped, the South Africans always started to camouflage their vehicles.

South African gunners were trained to put their rounds where the enemy turret meets the hull. But sometimes, if things went right, their shots penetrated elsewhere as well.

This big hole in the turret of an Angolan T-54/55 indicates that it had been penetrated by an Olifant 105 mm round.

looking for a way out. But not just *any* way; it had to be camouflaged to look like a glorious victory. It says a lot for his political talent that he saw one in the South African counteroffensive after their victory on the Lomba. And, therefore, on 15 November 1987 he decided on a risky new strategy, resting on three pillars:

- Firstly, he purposefully elevated the defence of Cuito Cuanavale to a heroic struggle of good against evil. He also vetoed all proposals to abandon the village and pull back to Menongue, and sent a Cuban tank tactical group (equivalent to a squadron) to stiffen FAPLA's spine. It would become a masterful propaganda war in which the perception was created that Cuito Cuanavale's defence resulted in racist South Africa's crushing defeat of the same magnitude as Nazi Germany's reverse at Stalingrad. This has since been eagerly disseminated by several academics and politicians, including those in the South African governing African National Congress.
- In the second place, he made contact with the American and the South African governments (the latter through its permanent diplomatic representative at the United Nations in New York). Castro let it be known that he was interested in peace talks. This, please note, was *before* the moves described immediately hereafter. His basic objective was to establish Cuba's political importance in any peace process, and that he had to be engaged if there was to be peace.
- Lastly, the Cuban leader came with a strategic and operational masterstroke. In order to bolster his peace overtures, he sent his crack 50th division (without consulting Gorbachev, who was rather miffed) to southwestern Angola. There this elite formation, under the command of Brigadier-General Patricio de la Guardia Font, started advancing southwards in the province of Cunene towards the Namibian border. This advance came *after* the SADF pulled back its main force from Tumpo, so that Cuban and Angolan claims that the South Africans at Tumpo was surrounded or cut off, is devoid of all truth.

Nevertheless, it was a very intelligent move. The South Africans were understandably worried. What was Castro up to? Was he going to stop at the border, or was he going to invade SWA? South African Military Intelligence gave a considered opinion that an invasion was unlikely, but they, too, could not provide absolute certainty. And the Cubans deliberately kept both the Americans and the South Africans guessing. (Keep in mind that the SADF's conventional units by this time had been pulled back to SWA or even South Africa proper, and that they had nothing more than the light infantry counterinsurgency units in the north of the territory to counter a Cuban thrust across the border.)

So the SADF hastily had to prepare for a worst-case scenario. Roland de Vries, arguably the SADF's most able mechanised warfare proponent, was called back from his command at the Military College in Voortrekkerhoogte and made second in command of a new formation, known as 10 Division, in order to dissuade the Cubans from doing anything rash. The new division was under the command of Brigadier Chris Serfontein, who was also OC Sector 10 in Ovamboland. As such, Serfontein was also responsible for the counterinsurgency effort against SWAPO, and he therefore gave de Vries more or less a free hand. De Vries assembled a mechanised division with tanks, armoured cars, mechanised infantry and artillery and prepared a very warm welcome for the Cubans, should these cross the border. He planned to pull back his forces to the vicinity of Tsumeb, evacuate the white population and engage the Cubans here on terrain of his choice in a mobile battle. Having defeated them, the idea was to start a counteroffensive and pursue them well into Angola.

Of course, it never came to that. Castro's purpose was to get *out* of the war, not to get sucked *deeper in*. And after the war it also became clear that Castro was afraid of the South Africans' nuclear bombs, of which there were six ready, with a seventh under construction. Their purpose was deterrence only, which seems to have been successful.

A double-barrelled Angolan ZSU-23 anti-aircraft gun. This rapid-fire weapon was greatly feared by the South Africans, as it penetrated the Ratel's armour with the greatest ease. Several SADF casualties were caused by this efficient weapon.

A South African tank transporter (note the number plate with the "R", indicating an SADF military vehicle) pulling an Olifant at Mavinga in 1987.

Clashes

The first ships and air freighters, full of troops, weapons and supplies, left Havana on 24 November 1987. By the end of January about 3 500 soldiers were in Cunene province and started moving southwards slowly as part of what they called *Operation Maniobra XXXI Aniversario*. In the first week of March, the build-up was far enough for some aggression to be shown, and a brigade with 40 T-62 tanks – better armoured and armed than the T-54/55s with which the SADF had hitherto tangled, reached the town of Chibemba. South African military intelligence got wind of the Cuban move halfway through April, and by the end of the month, the CIA informed the SADF that there were now some 13 300 Cuban troops in Cunene. By late May the division, organised in three task forces and with about 200 tanks, were firmly established in the south of the

province. In deference to the considerable firepower of the SAAF, they were heavily equipped with anti-aircraft weapons. Facing them was 10 SA Division, with perhaps 10 000 men and 50 tanks.

At the same time, the airstrips at the towns of Cahama and Xangongo were rebuilt so that they could house MiG-23 and MiG-21 fighter-bombers. This placed the Cuban air support within striking distance of South African bases south of the border, including Ruacana, Oshakati and Ondangwa.

Castro himself explained after the war

> that you should not undertake decisive battles on terrain chosen by the enemy; you must wage decisive battles when you choose the terrain and strike the enemy in sensitive and genuinely strategic spots. … The main idea was to stop them at Cuito Cuanavale and attack them from the southwest. Enough troops were gathered to seriously threaten points of strategic importance for South Africa and strike hard at them on terrain the we, and not the enemy, had chosen.[34]

The first clash between the Cubans and South African troops, engaged in a fairly routine hot pursuit of SWAPO guerrillas, took place on 18 April. The South Africans, used to the enemy usually retreating, were taken aback by the Cubans' aggressive posture. It dawned on them that a potential far more ominous chapter of the Border War could be about to be written. On 5 May, a force from 101 Battalion ran into a Cuban ambush. The 101 men gave as good as they got – killing 54 Cubans for the loss of 7 of their own – but a South African, rifleman Johan Papenfus, fell in Cuban hands.

South African special force teams were now inserted to gather intelligence. They came back with the news that the Cubans were

34 Isaac Deutschmann (ed.): *Changing the History of Africa* (Melbourne, Ocean, 1989), pp. 109-110, speech by Fidel Castro, 5.12.1988.

UNIIA light infantry being excercised before an attack early in 1988.

The same tank transporter, photographed from a different angle.

This is how it looks when a *plofadder* is exploded. This weapon looks like a garden hose full of explosives. It is fired with a small rocket at the one end to fall across a minefield and brought to explosion in order to blast a path through the mine field.

The same *plofadder* explosion a fraction of a second later.

Brothers in arms – a UNITA soldier with a South African colleague in front of a tank.

stationed in force at Techipa. A small force of 32 Battalion troops clashed with these Cubans, but had literally to run for their lives all the way to Ruacana on the border after their vehicles were destroyed. Another sharp engagement persuaded the Cubans to recoil to Xangongo.

In the meantime, enough SADF reinforcements – including 61 Mech and its organic tank squadron – arrived on the scene, and the South Africans decided to draw the Cubans out and give them a good hiding. Towards last light on 26 June, light Impala jet bombers took off from Ondangwa Air Force Base to simulate a strike on Techipa. As soon as the Cuban radar picked them up, they dove again beneath the horizon, and the South Africans released weather balloons, which registered as aircraft on the Cuban radar screens. The Cubans promptly launched six SA-6 missiles, allowing the South Africans to accurately plot their positions. The SADF artillery then mercilessly pounded the Cubans for six horrible hours, killing many of them. The South Africans' hope was for a Cuban counterattack, which would then run into an ambush. But the bombardment was so successful that none was forthcoming. Somewhat disappointed, the South Africans withdrew.

But in Havana Castro blew his top. He ordered his officers to respond vigorously. The next day, three armoured columns raced from Techipa towards Calueque. One of them clashed heavily with elements of 61 Mech and 32 Battalion. Two SADF Ratels were destroyed and one young officer was killed, while the Cubans lost two tanks, two armoured cars and eight trucks. The other two Cuban columns tried to outflank the South Africans, but were flung back with considerable loss by the South African artillery.

Later that afternoon, seven MiG-23s attacked the South African positions at Calueque for the first time from a low height. One

A Ratel-20 in Angola. Note the density of the bush.

bomb exploded between two Buffel vehicles, killing 12 soldiers and causing considerable alarm in South Africa itself. Two aircraft were hit by the defenders' fire, and one crashed on the way home. But, as an experienced South African trooper reported:

We had never been bombed like this by enemy aircraft in Angola. They shot with continuing accuracy and wanted to cause as much damage as possible. It felt like an eternity, and the MiGs turned again and again and came back to us standing next to the dam wall. They hit the dam wall with bombs, which fell left and right of us. Their 23 mm cannon moved us and shots rang out left and right of us. …

Slowly and shivering, full of dust, we crawled from under the Ratels. We started running and saw the damage caused. I do not

A captured FAPLA tank plough, designed to explode mines before the tank rides over them. The SADF also had similar vehicles.

believe that any South African force or groups had been attacked so aggressively before by the enemy's aircraft.[35]

This was the final, bloody spasm of the war. Both sides realised that they stood on the verge of a devastating all-out war which neither wanted or could afford. Besides, peace talks were already underway. A tacit agreement was reached not to escalate the fighting. The war was over, bar the shouting.

War in the air

One of the reasons sometimes advanced for the South Africans' inability to land a knock-out blow to their enemy, is the Cuban-Angolan mastery of the air. South African ex-minister and ANC stalwart Ronnie Kasrils, for instance, wrote about the last phase of the war: "Soviet MiG-23s had demonstrated their superiority over South Africa's aged Mirage fighters and now that they commanded the skies the network of SADF bases in northern Namibia was at their mercy."[36] Other writers also refer to the MiG-23's superiority in the air.

It is certainly a fact that the enemy dominated the air in the latter stages of the campaign. But this had very little to do with the purported superiority of the MiG-23 over the SAAF's Mirage F1 and everything with geography. The South Africans had two air force bases near enough to the battlefields around the Lomba, Chambinga and the Tumpo triangle to be of use. These were Rundu (on the Angolan border) and Grootfontein (around 250 km south of the border). The problem with Rundu was that the runway was too

35 Quoted in Scholtz: *The SADF in the Border War*, p. 381.
36 Ronnie Kasrils: "Turning point at Cuito Cuanavale" (*Sunday Independent*, 23.3.2008).

short to enable heavily-laden bombers from taking off there. This made this base only useful when returning home with a shortage of fuel – in other words, in emergencies. The SAAF was in the process of lengthening the runway, but the work was far from finished. Therefore, the bombers had to fly all the way from Grootfontein some 500 km to Tumpo and then back again. While the fighting raged around the Lomba, this was not unsurmountable. But as the battles moved northwards, the distance became a big problem. In the last weeks, the South Africans' time over target was no more than a minute or two.

Conversely, the further northwards the fighting moved, the easier things became for the Cuban and Angolan aircraft. These were based at Menongue, only nine minutes flying away from Tumpo. Which meant that they could loiter above the battlefield for up to an hour, looking for targets of opportunity.

No wonder the skies often seemed empty of SAAF aircraft, while the Cubans and Angolans roamed at will.

The fact is that the MiG-23 and the Mirage F1 were completely different animals. The Mirage was nimble and very manoeuvrable, being designed as a "dog-fighter", compared to the unwieldy MiG-23. The latter was meant as an interceptor of NATO bombers, meant to make a single fast, slashing attack and then clearing off. As such, it was faster than the Mirage, and it also accelerated faster. It had a better radar, being able to launch radar-guided missiles from the front. The Mirage had to make do with heat-guided missiles which could only be fired from behind. And, to make things worse, these right through the war never worked as advertised; they either flopped completely or exploded in the hot plume behind the enemy aircraft's jet engine. The two SAAF "kills" of MiG-21s in 1981 and 1982 (both by Johan Rankin), were done the old-fashioned way

Another view of the Angolan tank plough.

A destroyed, dug-in T-54/55 about to be towed out by an Olifant.

A third view of the same.

with the Mirage's twin 30 mm cannon.

Also, the South African fighter pilots were much better in the air than their counterparts. They were trained to operate independently and make their own decisions instantly, depending on the situation they encountered. The Cubans and Angolans operated under Russian rules, being strictly controlled from the ground and not allowed any independence of action.

This is borne out by the four encounters between SAAF and Cuban fighters during the Battle of Cuito Cuanavale:

- On 10 September 1987 a force of 10 MiG-23s were intercepted by 4 Mirages. One Mirage launched two Matra 550 heat-seeking missiles which tracked beautifully, but exploded prematurely. The MiGs fled.
- On 27 September, six Mirages were attacked from the front by MiGs. One of the radar-guided missiles exploded alongside Captain Arthur Piercy's Mirage and caused the hydraulic fluid to leak out. In a superb piece of flying, Piercy nursed his aircraft to Rundu, but as he had no brakes, he went off the far end of the short runway and was accidentally catapulted into the air by his ejection seat. He broke his back and lived on as a paraplegic. The aircraft, though heavily damaged, was repaired and flew again.
- On 24 February 1988, three Mirages were intercepted by MiG-23s. The SAAF pilots immediately attacked, and the MiGs fled.

- Later the same day, some Mirages on a bombing mission were again intercepted by MiG-23s. The South Africans wasted no time and attacked, but the MiGs fled and, due to their greater speed, could not be overtaken.

This short overview clearly show that one cannot speak of either the Mirage or the MiG being either superior or inferior to the other; they were merely different, each having their strengths and weaknesses. The SAAF's advantage lay with the men inside the cockpit.

In any case, all through the campaign (with the exception of the very last Cuban attack on 27 July 1988), enemy air attacks were invariably delivered from several thousand feet up and very inaccurate. Before 27 July, when 12 soldiers died, the South Africans lost exactly 4 dead as a result of Cuban or Angolan air strikes. In return, the enemy lost 8 MiG-23s, 4 MiG-21s and 2 Sukhoi-22s by SADF and UNITA ground fire.

Nevertheless, it is true that enemy bombing raids did hamper South African ground movements, even though special forces operators monitoring Menongue airbase warned the South Africans every time a gaggle of MiGs took off from there. Especially the artillerymen had to stop firing and pull camouflage nets over their guns every time, depriving their comrades of artillery support. It is equally true that the South African Army had a very effective drill against enemy air attacks, which mostly worked quite well. It was called *visgraat* (Afrikaans for "fish-bone"), used as a verb. When a convoy became aware of a possible strike from the air, the vehicles would *visgraat* – scatter to either side of the road and hide under trees or bushes, where they would be invisible to fast-moving jet bombers. This drill was practised relentlessly and saved many lives.

On the other hand, the SAAF aircraft could only carry out raids when they had a definite target. With their "toss-bombing" technique, also used by the British in the Falkland War, they usually successfully evaded the strong enemy anti-aircraft defences. The South Africans lost two aircraft – a Mirage and a Bosbok light spotter – to enemy ground-to air missiles, while a second Mirage was lost due to unknown reasons, either technical failure or as a result of enemy anti-aircraft fire.

Peace talks

We need not devote much attention to the peace talks. The first meeting between South African, Cuban and Angolan representatives – with US senior diplomat Chester Crocker as facilitator – took

The SADF Olifant squadron after having arrived at Mavinga in October 1987.

Three Olifant tanks in the dense Angolan bush. At times, the density made operations simply impossible.

Another view of the Olifants' arrival at Mavinga.

place in a London hotel on 3 and 4 May 1988. The meeting chiefly served to sniff at each other, as dogs do when first meeting. Nothing was decided, except to meet again.

A notable aside was that General Ulises Rosales del Toro, Chief of the Cuban Armed Forces, cornered his SADF counterpart, General Jannie Geldenhuys, and tried to intimidate him, threatening a massive Cuban invasion in SWA. Geldenhuys, no doubt having read his intelligence people's assessment about the unlikeliness of a Cuban invasion, refused to be cowed and gave as good as he got. The two clearly achieved a grudging mutual respect.

Ten days later, the South Africans met the Angolans separately in Brazzaville, and from the minutes one could see a certain flexibility among the MPLA representatives. The third meeting took place on 24 and 25 June in Cairo. On the first day, the chief Cuban

negotiator, Jorge Risquet, launched a furious attack on the South Africans, refusing to discuss the Cuban military presence in Angola and calling the South African proposals "a tasteless joke". An angry Pik Botha, South African Minister of Foreign Affairs, derisively countered the attack. For a moment, the talks seemed to totter on the brink of a precipice, but then Crocker adjourned the meeting. During the evening, a senior Russian diplomat hanging around in the wings apparently spoke to Risquet, and the next day it was a completely different story. The combative Risquet stayed silent.

When the next meeting took place, on 11 and 12 July in New York, it was a completely different story. Risquet was left at home and his place was taken by the urbane, soft-spoken Carlos Aldana Escalante. During this meeting, Aldana – for the first time ever – conceded a key South African and US demand, that Cuban troops

During one SADF attack, the breech of a 105 mm Olifant gun burst. The result was not pretty.

leave Angola in return for the South Africans pulling out of Angola and allowing UN Security Council Resolution 435 (providing for free elections in preparation of SWA becoming an independent Namibia) to be implemented. This was the key which swung open the door to peace.

Several more meetings took place, and it would be an exaggeration to say that it was plain sailing from here on. But all sides clearly displayed the political will to reach an agreement. The New York Accord was finally signed on 22 December 1988. The war was over.

CHAPTER 7
SO, WHO WON?

The years since the end of the Border War has been characterised by another intense battle, this time fought with words, not with weapons. The main stake was, very simply, who actually won?

The first shots of this war was fired by Fidel Castro, a real master of propaganda. Even before the shooting on the battlefield ended, he carefully started crafting a narrative which would become widely accepted. In May 1988 he gave the Non-Aligned Summit in Havana a version of events which is even today, in broad terms, faithfully preached by his disciples:

The battle and its outcome are of historic importance. More than six months have passed and they are far from taking Cuito Cuanavale, and they will not be able to take Cuito Cuanavale. There has been a total change in the balance of power. It is very important to know about this in order to answer a question which many people have in mind: Why does South Africa want to negotiate?

South Africa wants to negotiate because it is fighting a very strong force, one it had never encountered anywhere before. This is not 1975. The enemy had not been given one single chance. If they had taken Cuito Cuanavale and had annihilated the concentration of troops, what kind of negotiations could we have? We would have to sit down and accept the conditions they would have imposed on us. But this was impossible – everything has changed.[37]

Castro even went further, boasting that after the final three SADF attacks on Tumpo, "South Africa showed fear and began to refuse to fight ... From now on the history of Africa will have to be written before and after Cuito Cuanavale."[38]

37 Deutschmann: "Preface", in Deutschmann (ed.): *Changing the History of Africa*, p. viii.
38 Quoted in Willem Steenkamp: *South Africa's Border War 1966-1989* (Gibraltar, Ashanti, 1990), p. 163.

The results of the MiGs' bombing on that last day of the fighting may be seen clearly.

The holes made by the Cuban bombs on the Calueque dam wall.

Although even respected historians like US Professor Piero Gleijeses[39] have accepted Castro's narrative down to the last detail, this cannot be an excuse not to re-examine the facts independently. This chapter is an attempt to do just that.

39 See his *Visions of Freedom. Havana, Washington, Pretoria and the Struggle for Southern Africa* (Chapel Hill, University of North Carolina Press, 2014).

Before we go on, there is one other question which must be addressed. Some people, especially on the SADF side, deny that there ever was a "Battle of Cuito Cuanavale", and that the South Africans, therefore, could not have lost. This sounds pretty disingenious to me. While it is true that there never was fighting in the streets of Cuito Cuanavale, a tiny village, the Battle of Waterloo (1815) also

The wall of the Calueque dam which was damaged on 26 June, 1988.

The pipeline with which water was pumped from the Calueque dam to northern South West Africa was also damaged in the Cuban air strike.

A SADF tank transporter pulling a tank recovery vehicle at Mavinga in 1987.

A convoy of Olifants and Ratels crossing a shona.

was not fought in the streets of that Belgian town. Neither was the Battle of Leipzig (1813) fought within the confines of that city, nor did either of the Battles of Sedan (1870 and 1941) take place in that French village. The simple fact is that every battle gets the name of a geographical location, mostly close to the battlefield. Naming this battle after Cuito Cuanavale is as good as any other you might think of. Let us not make something out of nothing.

The adversaries weighed

From a professional military point of view, there can be no doubt that the SADF was a formidable fighting machine. Their training was stern and tough, and there usually was little love lost between the trainees and the NCO instructors who mostly really came down hard on the troops. But, what you lose in sweat during training, you save in blood on the battlefield, as the saying goes. And this is part of what made the SADF such a ferocious attacking force when they tangled with any enemy.

The other part of the equation was that the combat officer corps, at least up to the level of Commandant or Colonel, were tactically and operationally superb. This applied especially to the mechanised warfare brotherhood around Roland de Vries, Pat McLoughlin, Paul Fouché, Chris Serfontein and others. Among the generals one name

stands out, that of Constand Viljoen. Every inch a soldier's soldier, a man who set the revision of the Army's outdated Second World War-vintage tactical and operational doctrine in motion when he became OC Military Academy in 1966. Most of the other generals had little understanding of modern mechanised warfare in the African context. This even applied to General Jannie Geldenhuys, Chief of the Defence Force (1985-'90), who, however, did have an excellent understanding of counterinsurgency warfare. His talents on the political front were also superb, as witnessed by the valuable role he played during the peace talks in 1988.

On the other side of the hill FAPLA was a shambolic, disorganised force, badly led and trained. The soldiers, more often than not pressed into service, had little understanding of the cause they were fighting for. As witnessed by Soviet advisors, they sometimes simply ran away when fighting against the South Africans. It is true that they, at times, fought tenaciously when in defensive mode. But there was not a single instance during the entire war in which they succesfully stood against a SADF attack after making contact. And the FAPLA officer corps, including the generals, were even worse. All major campaigns were commanded either by Soviet or Cuban generals.

The Cubans, of course, were a different kettle of fish altogether. Because Castro kept them mostly far away from the real fighting,

Tanks on the way to Angola and the front.

they gathered little tactical experience during the long years of the war. When they finally clashed with the South Africans in early 1988, these were taken aback by the Cubans' fighting spirit and aggressiveness, but this, coupled with their inexperience, made them rash and inclined to suffer far greater casualties than actually was necessary.

We will, of course, never know how a full-scale war between the Cubans and the South Africans would have gone. It is safe to say that the Cubans would have been a far harder nut to crack than FAPLA, and that the casualty figures on both sides would have been very high.

The role of the objective

One gets the distinct impression that some people's answer to the question who won, is dependent on their political persuasion. Those who tend to become nauseous when they hear the name of President PW Botha, will be inclined to agree that, as ANC stalwart Ronnie Kasrils put it, there is "no doubt whatsoever that an epic victory had been won over the apartheid military machine in that embattled country the previous year, constituting a historic turning point in the struggle for liberation".[40] Others, who feel revulsion at the name of Fidel Castro and his Communist dictatorship, reiterate that the SADF won hands down.

However, this book is not about weighing the moral worth of the Cuban dictatorship versus the South African apartheid system. Everyone is free to do that for himself. In this book we are concerned with nothing but the verifiable facts.

---

40 Ronnie Kasrils: "Turning point at Cuito Cuanavale" (*IOL News*, 23.3.2008, at http://www.iol.co.za/news/world/turning-point-at-cuito-cuanavale-1.393891#.Ve7iQBGqqko).

Let us, therefore, eschew political persuasions and try and use objective criteria when attempting to answer the question who won. The important question is: What did the adversaries want to achieve, and to what extent did they succeed?

The importance of this question is attested to by the viciousness of the verbal fight about the SADF's alleged attempt to occupy Cuito Cuanavale. Of course, if the SADF did want to take the village, and the defenders prevented that, the Cubans and Angolans may claim to have won a victory. If Cuito Cuanavale never was a South African objective, this claim becomes much harder to sustain.

The occupation of Cuito Cuanavale, was, of course, hotly discussed behind the SADF scenes. But this was in the context of the debate about taking FAPLA on either east of the Cuito or advancing to the west of the river. In the latter case, the village would have been taken from behind. And, according to the mobile doctrine formulated by Constand Viljoen, Roland de Vries and others, the occupation of territory would be important only while affording tactical advantage, never for its own sake. In the end, however, this unorthodox approach was discarded for the orthodox attack in the enemy's face east of the river. In this last context, there were isolated references in the SADF planning documents to Cuito Cuanavale as an objective, but only if the place fell into South African hands without a serious effort or casualties.

On the other hand, Major-General Chris Thirion, SADF Deputy Chief of Staff Intelligence, is quoted by US historian Piero Gleijeses as saying in an interview: "We started with essentially the same battle plan we used in 1985 – simply to stop the offensive, but our plans changed when everything went so well. It was decided, halfway through the battle, 'Let's take Cuito'!" But Thirion also

The RSM of 61 Mech, the legendary Sergeant-Major Kobus Kemp, saying goodbye to his men in 1988.

Two men standing in front of the SWAWEK dam in northern South West Africa.

added. "So the idea was to wait and let Cuito fall on its own."[41] The documentary evidence thus allows very little room for any other conclusion: Based on the SADF archival documents, one can safely say that the village did not seriously figure as an objective.

The South African military strategic objective was to keep UNITA alive as a fighting force in order to prevent SWAPO from infiltrating the Okavango and Caprivi areas south of the SWA border, and to limit the SWAPO insurgency as much as possible to Ovamboland. Nothing more and nothing less. True, the South Africans would have *liked* to split Angola in two, or to replace the MPLA government in Luanda with a UNITA one. But they were realistic enough to realise that they did not have the political or military strength to do it.

Translated on to the operational level, they first wanted to stop the FAPLA offensive from taking Mavinga and its airstrip. Having succeeded, President PW Botha then ordered a counteroffensive to prevent FAPLA from repeating in 1988 what was becoming a yearly excercise. Operationally and tactically, this was formulated in formal orders to either destroy FAPLA east of the Cuito, or to drive these back over the river. Then the river had to be mined heavily, turned over to UNITA, after which the South African troops would go back base.

These orders are available in the SANDF Documentation Centre for any academic who is interested in the truth.

In this, the South Africans succeeded for more than 90%. The FAPLA offensive was smashed, and the Angolans were driven back all the way to Tumpo, where they retained only a relatively small bridgehead. The fact that the attackers failed in the last three successive attacks is proof of their generals' tactical and operational ignorance, but the fact remains that they reached almost all their objectives. As a matter of fact, FAPLA could not repeat its offensive against UNITA until 1990, which the latter then beat off on its own. This, too, confirms that the SADF reached its strategic and operational objectives.

FAPLA, on the other hand, failed in every single one. One need say no more about them.

As for Castro, his purpose was clearly to wriggle out of a hopeless war while smelling of roses. He did this mainly through a propaganda offensive, planting the defence of Cuito Cuanavale in the public mind as a deed of heroic giants, fearlessly standing up to an overwhelming Satanic force. But he did it very intelligently. He accompanied the propaganda offensive with a very real march with a belligerent force down to the SWA border, setting off alarm bells all over South Africa. Today we know that he was posturing. Back then, SADF intelligence did not believe that he would cross the border, and the South Africans assembled a formidable force to counter him if he did.

But they couldn't *know*. And that uncertainty in the minds of the South African decision makers – that was what he was after. And he succeeded brilliantly. It allowed him to accede to the key US and South African demand, that the Cuban forces in Angola be pulled out, without losing an ounce of prestige. And although there is no proof, it seems logical that this march also helped to concentrate the South African minds during the peace talks.

The following conclusion, it seems, is based on the facts: South Africa won. The MPLA lost badly, but Angola at least won the prospect of peace. And Cuba won as well. Which means, in fact, that it was, in the end, a draw with which all sides could live.

---

41 Gleijeses: *Visions of Freedom*, pp. 398 and 403.